Soldier Poets of the 2nd British Infantry Division

An anthology of contemporary poems

Soldier Poets of the 2nd British Infantry Division

An anthology of contemporary poems

Bob Cook and Robin McDermott
Editors

Published by Dragoon Publications

A CIP catalogue record for this book is available from the British Library.

ISBN 978-0-9927780-3-3

Prepared and printed by:

York Publishing Services Ltd
64 Hallfield Road
Layerthorpe
York YO31 7ZQ

Tel: 01904 431213

Website: www.yps-publishing.co.uk

CONTENTS

FOREWORD

BUCKINGHAM PALACE

As Patron of the Kohima Educational Trust I was excited to hear The Second Division Museum & Memorial Trust's endeavour to publish a book of poems composed by those of the 2nd Division who defeated the Japanese Imperial Army at Kohima in 1944. Seeing the endeavour, sacrifice and grit through the words of the soldiers who fought and delivered this most pivotal of victories is both moving and engaging.

What the poems may lack in lyrical perfection and clarity of expression they make up for in the striking immediacy of their experience lived on Kohima Ridge. Some are written by those left still on that ridge and some with two generations of reflection between them and the events. Despite the great variety of sources and perspectives from those who lived through Kohima, they are unified by two threads of humour and sorrow.

This anthology is an exceptional tribute to the brave men of the 2nd Division who gave their tomorrow for our today.

PREFACE

Wikipedia defines a 'War Poet' as a poet who participates in a war and writes about his experiences, or a non-combatant who writes poems about war.

None of the men who wrote the poems in this book could be classed as well known in the sense of Sasson, Owen or Brooke from WW1. In fact those men were already poets but they also happened to be soldiers because of the war.

The poems in this book were written by ordinary men who, in the main, were soldiers of the British 2nd Infantry Division. But for the war, they may never have donned a uniform. As part of the 2nd Division, they went to stand firm against an implacable foe in the most difficult terrain, enduring the most dreadful weather conditions; they wrote about their experiences either at the time or in later life. And in so doing they earned for themselves the right to be referred to as Soldier Poets.

For the purist, many of these poems would not be considered poems at all but merely 'doggerel' or at best, verse. But to the men who wrote them, they represented the honour and respect in memory of their mates who fell beside them in the vicious hand to hand combat, or who were blown to bloody pieces by the bomb and grenade, during the fighting at Kohima and in Burma.

Some of the poems were written when the men were at leisure after rigorous jungle training merely to pass the time away. But in almost every case, the poems reflect the deepest feelings of men isolated from their loved ones, five thousand miles from home and with a very real prospect of never seeing those loved ones again.

The poems have been donated to the museum not in their own right, but amongst other items or tucked away inside the pocket of a tunic or folded inside a soldier's Pay Book. Many have been hidden away for 65 years without seeing the light of day, until now.

The 75th Anniversary of the Battle of Kohima is a fitting time to reveal and share this wonderful and unique collection of war poems. They provide a moving tribute to those soldiers who came home, as well as those less fortunate who lie forever in foreign soil. This book is a testimony to their sacrifice.

Brigadier (Retd) Greville Kenneth Bibby CBE
Chairman
Kohima Museum

ACKNOWLEDGMENTS

The poems contained in this book have been sourced almost exclusively from records held within the collections of the Kohima Museum. The vast majority of them have been published previously, either in other collections of poems, or in such organs as the 2nd British Infantry Divisional newsletter *Keynotes*[1], and the South East Asia Command Newspaper – *SEAC.* The editors are therefore very grateful to the many soldiers of the 2nd British Infantry Division who submitted their poems and verses to these organs, as it is doubtful whether many of them would have survived otherwise.

In addition to this, a significant number of these poems were either written anonymously, or where some detail has been recorded, it was often restricted to the initials of the author, or occasionally his rank with initials, e.g. *Cpl A.F.* In some cases, the Tactical Identification Number (TIN) of the battalion or

1. Many of the poems were published in the 2nd British Infantry Division's very own morale-boosting publication called *Keynotes.* It first appeared on the 1st March 1943, and as a fortnightly journal, its claim was to be "For You and Yours". To the 15000 or so men of the 2nd British Infantry Division, who were far from home and undergoing intensive training for the fierce jungle battles which lay ahead, it justified that claim for it cost just 2 annas (equal to about 2½d at 1944 prices), and it kept him in touch with events at home, told him what the rest of the Division was doing, and sometimes tried to make him laugh. Overall, it succeeded in maintaining a personal link between all members of the 2nd British Infantry Division through the many articles and stories it contained, as well as providing commentary on sporting events and reporting their results.

other unit has been given as well, such as *Pte S.M. of 47*. Sadly, all copies of the list of the Division's TINs, which would have been secret documents, will have been destroyed following operations, which now means that it is no longer possible to identify authors in this way. However, where there is a name associated with any poem, the fullest of credit is given to the author.

As part of their work in compiling this collection of poetry, and where sufficient detail exists for them to do so, the editors have made every effort to make contact with each of the original authors or their immediate descendants, in order to seek permission for the inclusion of their work in this book. However, as a consequence the passing of at least 75 years since most of the poems were written, the vast majority of the 'known' authors have proved impossible to track. In this regard, thanks are due to:

Fusilier John Done – 1st/8th Battalion Lancashire Fusiliers
Gunner Richard George – 99th (Royal Buckinghamshire Yeomanry) Field Regiment, Royal Artillery
Lance Corporal Stanley Birchall – 1st Battalion, Royal Welch Fusiliers
Bombardier Richard Chamberlain – 99th (Royal Buckinghamshire Yeomanry) Field Regiment, Royal Artillery
Private Raymond Street – 4th Battalion, The Queens Own Royal West Kent Regiment
Mr Robert Street
Mr Christopher Parkhurst

The last wartime edition of *Keynotes* was dated March 1944, following which it ceased production. In 1954, the Division having moved to Germany several years previously, *Keynotes* was resurrected and continued publication, albeit less frequently, until 2004, when the Division made its final move to Edinburgh with a changed role.

Ms Easterine Kire
Mrs Sylvia May
The Burma Star Association

Finally, for those pieces where the original authors are either untraceable because their work appears to have been previously published anonymously, or no longer contactable, the editors have taken some comfort from the fact that they were happy at the time for their work to appear publicly. They are therefore reassured in their decision to include them in this book, particularly in light of the fact that all proceeds from its sale will go towards the upkeep of the Kohima Museum, which exists in part to keep the memory of them and their comrades alive.

THE POEMS

Across the globe and through the ages, soldiers have sought to portray their feelings and thoughts about their particular battles through the power of the written word. For the generals and brigadiers, this tends to be in the form of great works explaining their grand strategic planning (and good books they are as well), although in doing so, many seem to gloss over the trials and tribulations of the soldier on the ground. Meanwhile, regimental and other unit war diaries recount the events of the day or week as they occurred, but in equally sparse detail, for while officers may be mentioned by name, the ordinary soldier is invariably referred to as an 'OR' (Other Rank) or 'BOR' (British Other Rank).

Thus the ordinary soldier was left to take up his pen and write his own story. George Macdonald Fraser wrote a riveting account of his time as a private in the 9th Bn Kings Own Border Regiment with the 17th (Black Cat) Indian Division, while John McCann of $1^{st}/8^{th}$ Lancashire Fusiliers with the 2nd (Crossed Keys) British Infantry Division produced several books on his experiences at Kohima and beyond. And Gordon Graham MC and Bar, of the Queens Own Cameron Highlanders, also with the 2nd British Infantry Division, wrote a gripping account of his experiences specifically at Kohima. To these may be added Martin Tarmey MC, a Lieutenant in the 2nd Reconnaissance Regiment, who wrote a fictionalised account of his experiences, but there can be no doubt that he was there.

These books proved to be quite successful and there are plenty of others. However, there are also many additional accounts, privately published by their authors and really intended for their own small circle of family and friends. The writing of many of these personal accounts has mostly taken place later in the life of the writers and in this respect has often been cathartic.

But as well as writing books and other accounts, soldiers wrote poems. Some managed to get them published in national publications, but for the most part, their path to a wider audience tended to be through inclusion in regimental or divisional newsletters. Sometimes the words were about loved ones; sometimes about fallen comrades and sometimes just about the situations, often humorous, that they found themselves in. For this book, the poems and verses included have been extracted from personal records that have been donated to the Kohima Museum over many years. As already noted, a significant number of them have been previously published in the Divisional Newsletter, *Keynotes*, and while the quality and rhyme of the verse may vary somewhat, the one aspect that runs constantly though all of these pieces is the sincerity of the words.

PART 1 – BEFORE INDIA

Upon the outbreak of the Second World War, the 2nd British Infantry Division was based in Aldershot, from which it was almost immediately deployed to France as part of the British Expeditionary Force (BEF). Units of the Division were subsequently engaged in numerous actions, and to illustrate this, two of the first Victoria Crosses of WW2 were won by soldiers of the Division.

- 2nd Lt Richard Annand – 2nd Battalion, Durham Light Infantry, won his Victoria Cross for actions over 15th & 16th May 1940.
- WO2 (CSM) George Gristock, 2nd Battalion, Royal Norfolk Regiment, won his Victoria Cross during actions on the 21st May 1940 – he later died of his wounds.

Despite this, no poetry that may have been penned by any member of the Division covering its actions during this period appears to have survived, and following its repatriation from Dunkirk, the Division was relocated to North & East Yorkshire where it was able to fill the gaps in its ranks from the regimental depots stationed in those areas. Thus, while there were no Yorkshire regiments in the 2nd British Infantry Division, there were plenty of Yorkshire men!

Again, very few poems appear to have been written by Divisional members at this time, although some were written after the end of the war. The Divisional Newsletter *Keynotes* was not then in existence which may account in part for this, but a more likely reason was probably that many of the troops could get home fairly regularly, meaning that they had other priorities on their minds, which in turn lessened any tendency towards introspection.

Following its stint guarding the North East coastline against possible invasion, during which it was re-equipped and retrained, the Division moved to the Cotswolds where, in short order, it was inspected by the King, followed by a visit from the Prime Minister. These were clear indications that the Division was soon to be shipped overseas and in early 1942, the 2nd British Infantry Division sailed from Liverpool and Greenock in the largest sea convoy of the war to date, to end up in Bombay, having sailed via the Cape of Good Hope, South Africa.

Two poems written before the Divisions departure for India are known to have survived, written by the Reverend Kenneth Parkhurst, Chaplain to the Royal Welch Fusiliers, whose prescience of what might lie ahead for those he served caused him to reflect on their behalf.

THE PADRE

The Padre's got a cushy job, he roams about all day
He doesn't work, he merely talks and wastes his time away
He wears his collar back to front and looks professional
But don't let him take you in he doesn't work at all

It's war boys, and we've got to fight, and that's our job for now:
The CO and the officers are here to tell us how
The MO's here to patch us up – we'll need him in this war-
But is there anybody who knows what the Padre's for?

The army must be mechanised if we're to make a show
And every Fusilier admits we want an MTO[1]
A Quartermaster there must be to superintend the store
But only the almighty knows just what the Padre's for

And yet I've just been thinking chaps, that surely, he was sent
To do a job of some kind, for he's not an ornament
I've heard it said by friends of mine who met a few in France
That Padres can come up to scratch if men give them a chance

I get my problems and my thoughts, I get temptations too
And secret fears I'd like to share with someone, Bill, don't you?
We're not the only ones like that, there must be many more
And so I've sometimes wondered if that's what the Padres for

Mind you, I'm not afraid to die, and I don't ask for fuss
But we've got girls or wives and kids who think the world of us
And if I get knocked out tonight and laid I don't know where
Although I'm not a churchy chap, I wouldn't mind a prayer

---

1. Mechanical Transport Officer.

Take that young fellow over there who's getting on so well –
If he gets shot his mother's heart is going to hurt like hell:
If Padre wrote it wouldn't bring him back, for nothing could
And yet she'd be relieved to know that someone understood

That someone understood, you know, someone who was nearby
Who lived with us, and knew his name, perhaps who saw him die
And every mother in the hour of bitterness and loss
Might like to know that someone tried to help her boy across

I've asked you what a Padre's for: well now, I wonder, Bill
If he's been sent by Jesus Christ to help us up the hill
He's not a saint and yet its grand, tho' some might think it odd
That we should have a fellow here to make us think of God

Reverend Kenneth W Parkhurst MBE HCF
Chaplain to 1st Battalion, Royal Welsh Fusiliers –
2nd British infantry Division.

BRITISH TOMMY

June 1940

They think he doesn't care because he whistles all the time
Because he marches with a swing and takes it with a smile
Because he makes a jest or two when others wouldn't dare
Because he sings and smokes his fags, they think he doesn't care

They think he doesn't care because his courage goes so deep
But he has thoughts you'll never know and tears he yearns to weep
And sometimes friendship's magic touch will rend the veil apart
And while he talks you'll wonder at the poet in his heart

They think he doesn't care and yet he carried in his coat
The photograph of someone and the letter that she wrote
And though he's not a saint of course, and needs a Saviours' grace,
When he talks about his laddie, I've seen Heaven in his face.

Reverend Kenneth W Parkhurst MBE HCF
Chaplain to 1st Battalion, Royal Welsh Fusiliers –
2nd British infantry Division.

DRILL[1] SQUARE

They are marching up and down, up and down, up and down.
And their feet are making echoes everywhere,
They are hardly more than boys and they're making such a noise
Just obeying orders on the square

They are thinking all the while, all the while, all the while,
Of the folk they left back home beside the fire
They are praying to be brave, when they're out across the wave[2],
Their hearts are just a fever of desire.

Up above them on a pole, on a pole, on a pole,
Is a coloured, crested, piece of linen rag
And they gaze with pride on high to their symbol in the sky
'Tis the emblem of their honour, 'tis the Flag.

---

1. Drill – the first collective introduction to discipline that a soldier encounters. Drill allows large bodies of men to move in unison in the same direction in a disciplined manner. Originally it enabled troops to be moved about the battlefield according to the commander's strategic plan. Drill instils discipline and encourages pride. Drill also allowed synchronized handling and firing of weapons.

   Incorporated into modern usage – "What's the drill?"; "Come on now, you know the drill".

2. Across the wave – overseas.

So they just obey and wheel on a nicely polished heel
All the training that they do is just a phase,
They are waiting for to go, rushing on their country's foe
In a moment that's the summit of their days

Leslie Sumsion
A Soldier in the 2nd British Infantry Division
Taken from *Keynotes* November 1943[3]

3. Although written in India, this poem is clearly about the initial training back in 'Dear old Blighty'.

PART 2 – ARAKAN 1943

Following its arrival in India in 1942, the 2nd Infantry Division – being the only completely British formation stationed there at that time – found itself somewhat 'unwelcome'. This was because it tended to have different requirements, not just culturally, but also in more tangible aspects such as food, pay and equipment. As an example of the last of these, the Division was mechanised and therefore considered to be restricted to operations using just the road system. As a result, these differences tended to set it apart from otherwise similar formations in the Indian Army. And while it had been intended for the Division to train for seaborne operations to retake Burma, the boats needed for this operation had been recalled back to the UK and the plan was shelved. So, in light of the political unrest and the food riots due to the famine in India at that time, the Division found itself being used for internal security purposes, providing yet further grounds for potential alienation.

It was thus against this background that the Division's 6th Brigade, commanded by Brigadier Ronald Valentine Cecil Cavendish OBE MC, was selected to be deployed as an Independent Infantry Brigade to the Arakan early in 1943. For this purpose it was placed in support of the 14th Indian Infantry Division, commanded by Major General Wilfrid Lewis Lloyd CBE, DSO and Bar, MC, to take part in what has since become known as the First Arakan Campaign, an operation which had been hastily put together in response to Burma falling to the Japanese in 1942.

However, the fact remained that the whole of the logistic framework of the British Indian army at that time was still inadequate in both currency and scale to provide effective support to such a campaign, and this was exacerbated by the emerging famine in West Bengal that had resulted in part from the Japanese occupation of Burma which prevented rice imports.

Nevertheless, in response to great pressure from Whitehall and Washington, the First Arakan Campaign was planned to try and restore the supply route to the Chinese in the north. If the Chinese fell to the Japanese, this would release almost 41 Japanese divisions to be deployed on the Indian and Pacific fronts which would change the whole outcome of the war in the Far East. Unfortunately, due to the very short timeframe and logistic shortfalls generally, it is clear in hindsight that this campaign was poorly planned and badly executed. As casualties mounted, more men were sent to the Arakan, until nine Brigades came under command of 14th Division. The fact is that neither Major General Lloyd, nor his staff were equipped in training or experience to handle nine Brigades at once on such a wide front in such terrain. The normal for his level of capability and staffing was just 3 Brigades. The British Eastern Army Commander, Lieutenant General Noel Irwin relieved him of his command[1] and briefly took control of the campaign himself. Then Lieutenant General Slim was sent forward to appraise the situation and advised withdrawal.

Following the failure of the Arakan campaign, in which the 6th Infantry Brigade, enhanced by the addition of 1st Battalion, Royal Scots (The Royal Regiment), had played a part, the 2nd British Infantry Division began extensive jungle training, using the very useful experience gained by 6th Infantry Brigade. And it was during this jungle training phase that the 'flow' of poems

1. Major General Lloyd was relieved of his command but was soon given another operational command. He was killed in a plane crash in January 1944.

appears to have started, underlined by the fact that this was when Lance Corporal Stanley Birchall, 1st Battalion, Royal Welch Fusiliers first took up his pen and wrote his collection of poems. A veteran of the Arakan Campaign, L/Cpl Birchall was later wounded at Kohima in 1944. He died of his wounds on 1st June that year and is buried in Imphal War Cemetery. Through this publication, we remember his sacrifice – for his poems pretty much tell the story of the failed 1943 Arakan Campaign.

> "This is an attempt to portray events as they happened during the battalion's campaign in Burma. The author himself makes no claim to be a poet, rather let it be said that these verses were attempted during periods in reserve, more for the author's own amusement than any attempt at literary gain.
>
> However, talks with various people who participated in this campaign have convinced him that these people are definitely interested, and so the verses have been arranged in order and are here for your perusal."

S Birchall – *Written by the author in the third person*

As the following 20 poems are taken from the collected works of Stanley Birchall, they receive no individual acknowledgement until the final poem.

DEDICATION

These verses with which we tell our story
Which are sometimes pleasant and sometimes gory
We're inspired by one who went by name
Of Walling of Orderly Room fame
So to this Walling they are dedicated
In the hope that when we have Burma vacated
They may be perused during moments of leisure
And afford the reader some measure of pleasure

JOURNEY TO DONBAIK –

4th – 9th March 1943

It was well before reveille
One very hot March day
And over hill and valley
We sweated, all the way
We rested by the jetty
Then went aboard the ship
And, still feeling rather sweaty
Began our little trip

Across the broad Naf river
We many a sampan saw
Then the ship with many a quiver
Tied up right by Maungdaw
Then we continued marching
Still feeling rather damp
And the sun, it sure was scorching
When we reached the staging camp

A day and a half we stayed there
And found a ration store
Twelve-man packs were laid there
And biscuits by the score
These rations were quite tasty
Marching all through the night
And being rather hasty
At each halt we'd snatch a bite

Mules were our means of transport
Ours a Barbary wallah
At the slightest thing, he'd bolt
And after him we'd follow
We reached our destination
The end of our long hike
And took up occupation
Of a valley near Donbaik

IN RESERVE

Although only a mile behind the line
Life in reserve was rather fine
We didn't hear much from Johnny Jap
So during the day we'd take a nap
Of course, we still had our duties to do
But these were easy and very few
So altogether behind the line
We had a rather pleasant time

FRONT LINE

13th – 18th March 1943

In the line we took our turn
Whilst overhead the sun would burn
Scorching every living thing
Even the birds were too hot to sing
And during the day along the line
Of the Jap, there was hardly a sign

There was every now and then a shot
But for real fighting it was too hot
The guns, they shelled him good and strong
Round Sugar Five[1] and along the Chaung[2]
Every now and then he'd have a smack
And his 75's[3] would begin to crack

And if at us his guns did fire
Into our dugouts we'd retire
But it didn't seem like a battle line
There was nothing to do most of the time
And so the days went rolling on
To the morning when our attack began.

---

1. Sugar Five is a target designation reference of a Japanese position.
2. Dry river bed.
3. Refers to the calibre of the Japanese artillery.

DONBAIK

18th March 1943

It is miles away across the sea
In the nullahs approaching Donbaik
Where they gave their lives for you and me
And fought and died for England's sake

At the crack of dawn artillery flashed
With salvo of shell upon shell
And under that barrage the lads were dashed
Straight into the mouth of hell

They reached their objective, where they fought
With rifle and bayonet and bomb
But on their objective, they were caught
By Jap mortars and machine guns

All day long 'neath the burning sun
Covered with blood, dust and sand
They stuck to their guns and they still fought on
In the midst of no man's land

And we that are left, how can we forget
Our comrades, so gallant and so true
Those Sons of Wales are with us yet
They'll be with us our whole life through

And now, to those comrades who have gone
We say that they died not in vain
What they began we shall still carry on
Till peace is back with us again

Until that freedom they died to get
Prevails upon this earth again
And we shall not need any "lest we forget"
For we shall remember them!

RELIEVED

18th March 1943

Lots of our wounded were still passing through
To R.A.P.[1] and to A.D.S.[2]
And out in the open were still quite a few
We tried to relieve them but without success

Then up came the Jocks[3], part of our Brigade
And took over positions we had left
And under cover of darkness they made
An attack, and the casualties swelled

They attacked Sugar Five and along the Chaung
But like us found no entrance there.
And while they were slinging grenade and bomb
The Jap brought his mortars to bear

So they retreated, and held a line
Whilst we, tired, dirty and dishevelled withdrew
To an area where we could rest for a time
In comparative quiet, and little to do.

---

1. Regimental Aid Post.
2. Advance Dressing Station.
3. 1st Battalion Royal Scots (The Royal Regiment).

REST AREA

19th – 23rd March 1943

We bathed there in the filthy stream
Washed our clothes and felt quite clean
After the blood and dust and sweat
Which in the front line we used to get
But over us all was a sense of gloom
Casualty lists in the Orderly Room

We thought of the men who'd been with us for so long
Meeting their deaths with a smile and a song
We wondered then, perhaps for the first time
Of how long we were to hold that line
And so we prepared to reorganise
And got ready to move back to the line and the flies.

HILL 566

23rd March – 4th April 1943

This time we carried our big packs
And blankets on our shoulders
And as up 566 we trekked
They felt like bloody boulders

So we trudged on, what a climb
Wet through with sweat we were
Believe me it took us quite a time
To reach our positions there

Once more we slept in dugouts
Once more we'd not to slack
Once more with round pushed up the spout
"Stood to" by a jungle track

And every morning come what may
Descend the hill we must
And draw our water for the day
Or else be parched with thirst

We stayed up there upon that hill
For days and days and days
Of 566 we had our fill
Line lost through illegibility on original poem

At tiffin time and again at tea
His 75's came over
Dugouts were used then and believe me
We really dived for cover

Then word came through that a force of japs
Had cut the road to Maungdaw
So once again we packed our traps
And began to prepare to be withdrawn

4th – 5th APRIL 1943

All day long, troops could be seen
Beginning to move back
Chosen as rear guard we had been
In case of Jap attacks

By darkness, all but us had gone
We held positions there,
But as the night rolled slowly on
We left him unaware

If he had known that we'd withdrawn
If his patrols had seen us –
Believe me, during night and dawn
We put many miles between us

All through the night we trudged along
In silence, grim and wary
This was no time to sing a song
No time to be light and airy

Then, with what cover we could find
Took up positions new
We'd Japs in front and Japs behind
A terrible 'how- do- you -do'

We tried to snatch a bit of rest
Brewed up char in a petrol tin
Then we continued on our quest
Of attacking at Indin.

TO INDIN STAGING CAMP

We trudged that dusty road along
En route for Indin Camp
The sun was burning fiercely strong
All that we wore was damp

And all along the road we saw
Vehicles and trucks parked there
Cut off they were from old Maungdaw
By guns the Japs had brought to bear

Our gunner, stripped to the waist,
Guns belching smoke and fire,
The natives packing up in haste
Preparing to retire

And to our flank upon the hill,
The Japs in position were,
So pouches with ammunition filled
And for attack prepare

And so those hills our lads attacked
Their morale was fairly stunning
They were by our artillery backed
But the Japs still proved cunning

To our right flank those Japs now moved
And infiltrating there,
And this their move successful proved
As we were soon aware

THE BATTLE OF INDIN

6th April 1943

That piercing shriek and ghastly yell
As the Japs attacked, I remember well
It broke the stillness of the night
And made our hair stand up with fright

Just eight of us lying there
Thank heavens the Japs were unaware
Or else, I am afraid to say
We wouldn't have seen another day

It can now be fairly stated
We simply held our breath and waited
Up the breech a round we slammed
Grenades in plenty, near at hand

The Japs passed on – our hopes arose
But still we waited on our toes
Brigade HQ, they then perceived
And what a bashing it received

To companies went an SOS
To come and clear this bloody mess
And so throughout that long, long night
We waited there, prepared to fight
Knowing that if we were spotted
Our copy books would be rather blotted

Morning came and not too soon
For throughout the night there'd been no moon
His 75's began to shower
We were heavily shelled for about an hour
And he obtained a direct hit
On the mortar ammunition pit

This killed eight mules, bloody bits flew around
And blood was splattered on the ground
But a force of Japs could now be seen
Using a wood there for a screen

Gosh, did we give them merry hell
With mortar fire, LMG's[1] as well
A hail of bullets thick and fast
Against such fire, they couldn't last

They scattered here, they scattered there,
Those Japs, they scattered everywhere
But they never could get beyond
Our range of fire and mortar bomb
But alas, they'd gone and done their damage
For they were more than we could manage
And so, before it was too late
We began to evacuate

1. LMG – Light Machine Gun.

And so we hurried down to the beach
His 75's to get out of reach
One or two did fall around
But failed to explode in the boggy ground

His MG's to begin to splutter
And many a prayer our lads did utter
We kept plodding on, just doing our best
For we dare not stop to have a rest

Full well we knew that speed would tell
So just kept on, pushing like hell
And all along the beach there lay
Bits of kit that had been thrown away

But then is it a crime to forsake
Your kit when your lives are all at stake?
And ambulances patrol the sand
Taking the wounded and giving a hand

Drinks of water they gave to us
Like manna from heaven, I'll say it was!
And then at last we'd reached our goal
And found we'd won through after all

How sweet it was to have a rest
To wash and shave and to feel refreshed.

REACTION AND LONGING

I must get back from the Front again
From this hellish Front, and the bloody Jap
Away from long hours of "Standing to"
With never a chance of having a nap
All I ask is a good long sleep and lots of laughter
A nice cool bath with clean clothes after

I must get out of the sun again
From this scorching sun and choking dust
From the burning rays, the long day through
Oh God, return I must

All I ask is a shady bank
With green leaves overhead
And long grass, with a cool breeze
Playing round my head

All I ask is a peaceful scene
Where birds are singing
The countryside in bloom
And church bells ringing

I must get to my home again
To the peace of the old fireside
To a mother's care and a father's joy
And for the pleasure in their eye

To the life I led in the days of yore
Before the dreadful war began
I want to get to that home again
But only when victory is won.

MORE SHELLS

Now once again we took a rest
For we'd fought hard and done our best
And as we'd missed many nights sleep
We were soon wrapped up in slumbers deep

Planes flew around and flares they dropped
The guns did roar and they hardly stopped
But we remained in sweet repose
Whilst other troops held back our foes

And then we learned that in the fight
At Indin camp that hellish night
Our Brigadier[1] and most of his staff
For prisoners had been carried off.

Reorganised, we formed a line
But we were feeling far from fine
Full well we knew that fight we must
Repelling Japs with all our might

And once again he got our range
And shell for shell we did exchange
Believe me, hell is mighty hot
And makes you feel most every shot

---

1. Brigadier Ronald Valentine Cecil Cavendish, OBE, MC
Thought to have been killed in action by Allied artillery.

And poor Brigade got it again
In both materials and men
And as his troops were closer drawing
We talked again of our withdrawing

And once again we began to fear
That the Japs would come up in our rear
And this they did, and well we saw
Once more we were cut off from Maungdaw

FURTHER WITHDRAWALS

As we "stood to"[1], boy, did it rain!
But we "stood to" there just the same
And got soaked through right to the skin,
And we'd only the clothes that we stood in

At "stand down" we searched around
To see if shelter could be found
But our search was fruitless
And we just crouched there – what a mess!

At dead of night we formed up there,
In another withdrawal, we had to share.
And in silence on our way
Along the beach close by the spray.

The Japs knew not that we'd departed,
We hardly stopped when once we'd started.
And so, from beach along the road
We march along, a silent horde.

For hours and hours we marched
Wet through with sweat, and throats were parched.
Eventually we got a rest
And went to kip there fully dressed.

---

1. Short for 'Stand to Arms', which was observed by both sides in WW1 trench warfare, in expectation of an attack. Stand to Arms lasted for between an hour and an hour and a half at dawn and again at dusk. Stand down was the reversal.

A couple of hours, and up again,
This time conveyed by MT[2] train
To a valley by a chaung
Low lying hills running along

There we stayed in reserve again
Snatch some rest, ye war weary men

2. Mechanical Transport.

DONAPARA

Here we tried to sort things out,
During past weeks, we'd been knocked about.
And of course, we still had a shortage of kit
But we got some clean clothes, though they didn't fit

And of course, we still did our stag[1] every night
But really our duties were rather slight
So we managed to get a much-needed rest
But were still feeling far from our best

Then they decided to shorten the line
So we had to retire, and we rode this time
And took up positions again in the rear
Oh, why can't we leave, and from Burma get clear?

1. To be on stag – a military term – to be on guard duty.

DILPARA

Here we stayed quite a while,
Behind the front by a couple of miles.
We sent out patrols and still did our stag,
We slept in our clothes, that was the snag.

Then we had our positions to make,
And quite a time the digging did take
Up in the hill a Company went
To help the Scots they had been sent[1]

And all the time the wily Jap
Was infiltrating and setting a trap.
So a Company went and took abode
On the Maungdaw-Buithidaung cross road
The Japs pushed on and soon we saw
That once again we had to withdraw

---

1. The 1st Battalion, The Royal Scots (The Royal Regiment).

WITHDRAWAL AGAIN

Again, at night we marched along,
Again, no jokes or bursts of song.
We passed the road down to Maungdaw
And lots of activity there we saw.
And all the time the guns they fired,
Holding the Japs while we retired.
All through the night we marched along,
Passing many a hill and chaung,
And took up positions for the day
Whilst many troops passed by our way.

TO TAUNGBRO

There we spent a couple of weeks,
Washing our clothes in tidal creeks
It sure was hot – we felt the sun
And that monsoon had not yet begun
And still the chaps went down "in dock"[1],
We sure have lost a tidy lot
Malaria had taken many
Of our company blokes there were hardly any.
At last we knew that we were going back
And leaving to others the Japs to crack
On truck and train we rolled along
Arriving eventually in Chittagong

1. In dock – a Naval expression. To be in dry-dock, in for repair – adapted to mean 'in hospital'.

BACK TO NAGAR

Again in India's sunny clime
We stayed in Chittagong for a time
But still we marched upon our way,
Along the road to the old jetty

Then on a ship for a day or two
We sailed across the sea so blue
At Calcutta we left the ship
And on the train continued our trip

Right across from East to West,
At times we were by heat oppressed
And as up Nagar's hill we climb
Cool breezes there we seemed to find

And from the train into the camp;
We made our beds by hurricane lamp
With Char Wallahs standing near the door,
And every day to have a shower
And know that our campaign is o'er.

Whilst training – Dedicated to Fusilier G Trivett

WET FEET

We formed up in serial on Mess decks
And sat there sweating like hell
Awaiting our call to the LCA's[1]
The call of the telephone bell

Then slowly we followed our leader,
This time to Sally Port Two
And slowly descended the scrambling nets
With another assault landing in view

Then dawn it had not yet broken
As we crouched in the boat on our toes.
We were hoping the beach had been taken
And been cleared of all mines, and our foes

With a splash we leapt into the water,
And cleared that beach mighty fine
And got under cover as soon as we could
For planes were around all the time

Slowly we began pushing forward,
Across paddy field among the shrub
Our faces were tense, our blood all on fire,
We didn't even think about grub

---

1. Landing craft army.

At length we cleared the whole island
The enemy were prisoners or dead
So the CO said "OK, scheme's[2] over.
Pack up and go back to bed

Lance Corporal Stanley Birchall –
1st Battalion, Royal Welsh Fusiliers

4204365 Lance Corporal Stanley Birchall is remembered here for his sacrifice

2. Scheme – training exercise.

THE BATTLE OF DONBAIK

March 1943

Have you heard of the fighting "6th Brigade"?
Their way to the Donbaik front they made
With orders from the 'Bara Sahib'[1]
To clear the way to Akyab

The 14 Div. with little sense[2]
Had never tested his defence
So the Welsh went over like herds of cattle
And lost their lives in a useless battle

They got right up to 'Sugar Five'
And found it very much alive
But the cunning Jap had shut the door
Then got right underneath the floor

He played a very crafty game
For from behind his mortars came
Old Jap was safe beneath the ground
But seen our chaps lay all around

---

1. This is a term to describe a high-ranking officer or public official. So in this case it is likely to be the Divisional or Brigade Commander.
2. Again the soldiers on the ground held Major General Lloyd – General Officer Commanding 14th Indian Infantry Division, responsible for the Arakan debacle. History has shown him to have been extremely overburdened without sufficient staff to fight with 9 brigades.

Some people were not satisfied
So again, this job had to be tried
In the still of the night our Company B
Took the test reinforced by D

Forward they crept all alert
Everyone knew; this would be no cert
Then hell let loose; they hadn't a chance
Old Jap again had stemmed the advance

For a while we had a quiet spell
Something was brewing, you could tell
Then came news of his cunning stunt
He'd attacked behind from Indin Front.

At 2am from the fields he came
Screaming and shouting the regiments name
"Come out Royal Scots, we know where you are"
And shouted the password "Coxs Bazaar".

Many a man prayed that night for dawn
But by that time some of their pals had gone
Jap's hopes of victory were very high
When up came the 'Welsh' and the 'DLI'

The enemy cornered in some huts
Battered from our heavies they lost their guts
And so, coming out with a flag of truce,
They fell like corn when we let loose

Then withdrawal along the beach
For the Hopkins Defence, we had to reach
Along they came in single file
Tired; but they knew it had been worth while

But there is one brain I must admire
Amid this hell and rapid fire
For as the shells and bullets did hum
Up came our QM with our ration of rum[3]

When reading this it sounds as if
This was the end of our little tiff
But the 6th Brigade were soon to know
It was just a phase in our Burma show

Written by J Cosgrave
Saddler
1st Battalion, the Royal Scots (The Royal Regiment)

---

3. Soldiers were issued rum in extremely cold weather or on active service. Supposedly carefully rationed as it was a very potent drink.

RHQ[1] – Arakan April 1943

I am a famous General[2]
I work in big divisions
With singular ability
I make my wise decisions
I ride about in a car so fine
With red upon my cap
And though I'm not with the boys in the line
I've got them on my map

Remember, men, the things I've said
In all my perorations
I have a bright new pin or two to mark your battle stations
And when you start the big attack
You mustn't mind a scrap
Although I am a long way back
I have you on my map

Whatever happens, pray be calm
By nothing I'm confounded
It really doesn't matter much
If your unit gets surrounded
We'll think of you in jungle deep
And don't get in a flap
Whatever happens, I shall keep
You fellows on my map

---

1. RHQ – Regimental Headquarters.
2. It may be that the 'General' referred to in the poem above is the already mentioned Major-General Wilfrid Lewis Lloyd CBE, DSO and Bar, MC or Lieutenant General Noel Mackintosh Stuart Irwin CB, DSO and two Bars, MC.

I never get the sickening fear
That grips you in the belly
For things appear so different
From an office, back in Delhi
If no supplies this week you see
Don't think you're in a trap
Bravo! You fellows "ectually"
I have you on my map

Crack on, you British troops, crack on
And get to know your jungle
I count on you to do your stuff,
You count on me to bungle
And if ever you go to Tokyo
In the hands of a little Jap
It'll comfort you very much to know
That I had you on my map!

Reverend Kenneth W Parkhurst MBE HCF
Chaplain to 1st Battalion Royal Welsh Fusiliers –
2nd British Infantry Division

JUNGLE ATTACK – OCTOBER 1943

Then to attack; hell, madness in the reek
Of swamp; and tortured agony of hands
So strangely thick with blood. What did they seek
A while ago – but things remote as strands
Of shining hair, or hearts construction
But that is now no more. They are as mad
As screaming lead or guns destruction,
Or the bayonets sickening jab……

And we would search, and find the fallen ones
Amid the awful gloom, among the roots
Of twisted trees, and the brackish scum
Of stinking mud; and the endless shoots of creepers
Then we would feel – feel for their
Very blood, sticky and warm, and messing
Broken limbs. Ah, stop the flow, repair,
And then apply the first field-dressing

Get them away; back to the clearing stage
Immune to all their pain, and stabbing ache
Another load, another priceless wage
But mammon and his lust, we never slake
I knew this man – we carry now, a strong
And vigorous life – built like a horse
The singing loud, an old familiar song
Sounding a little crude – a little coarse.

I did not notice how his singing grew –
Dim as we passed beneath the tangled bough
That's how he went, to join the other crew –
This on his lips, "I wonder who's kissing her now"

Quietly his great red life had poured away
No boom of gun, no carillon of hell;
No solemn note, but childlike, richly gay
The singing died and dying, could not tell.

Gunner Richard George,
99th (Royal Buckinghamshire Yeomanry) Field Regiment
Royal Artillery[1].

1. This regiment also fought in the 1943 Arakan Campaign.

NO MAN'S LAND

The tropical sun blazed down from the cloudless sky.
Vultures hovering in their increasing numbers where khaki clad lie
Flies swarm as if in a maze, bodies warm in the mid-day haze

Figures depicting ballet dancers as in pose,
Japs all around, so near, so close.
With binoculars I observe men as if asleep.
Carrion glide on high searching the terrain with hungry eye.

Khaki figures attempt to creep from the carnage grave,
Each movement excruciating pain.
I avert my glance to a Khaki figure to the fore creeping stealthy on all fours.
Sudden spurts of dust erupt on either side of him, the slant eyes have espied him.

Transfixion he maintains no doubt his body racked with pain.
Here in my O.P[1]. I uttered 'Why'? looking to heaven, I begin to cry
The only release appears to me, is when the sun disappears beneath the sea

When night falls I shall descend, hoping and praying to save my friend.
As I observe my friend as if dead, he suddenly stiffens and relaxes in a heap.
Peace at last he is asleep, no more he needs to creep.

---

1. Observation Post.

From the Japs further shots ensuring my friend is pinned to the spot.
Mental exhaustion I'm overcome, my whole body becomes numb.
I must escape before it's too late, in order to avoid my friends fate.
Goodbye friend I must be off, to where sanity reigns, that's my lot.

Arthur Cordingley
6th Brigade, 2nd British Infantry Division, Royal Signals
Arakan, Kohima 1943

PART 3 – BEFORE KOHIMA

After the Arakan, the 2nd British Infantry Division, like the remainder of the 14th Army, entered a period of intensive training. The lessons provided by 6th Brigade's experiences were taught to the remainder of the Division and the men learned quickly. Despite the relentless training, there was still plenty of time for courses, leave and entertainment. The soldiers also had time to reflect and for many this meant putting pen to paper. Accordingly, they were encouraged to submit letters and articles to publications produced by the various military commands, in particular the newly published Divisional newsletter *Keynotes*, as well as *SEAC,* the South East Asia Command Newsletter. They were often paid small sums for such contributions, and the enthusiasm this generated soon led to the introduction of a 'Poets Corner'. The poem below is one such.

THE BULLOCK

Placid, remote from the world's stress and strife
Peacefully plodding along in the dust,
Carrying cheerfully all that you must
Bearing the burden of India's life

Knowing no pleasures beyond food and rest,
The winds soft caress, the shade of the trees
Knowing no sorrows save absence of these,
No seething passions at war in your breast.

Hitched to the plough, or the slow creaking cart,
Or, drawing up water, you have the art,
The gift that is priceless, exceedingly rare
Of living contentedly free from all care

Oh Brother oxen, I would I could be
Peaceful and placid, contented as ye.

J. W. N.
Taken from *Keynotes*
A Soldier of the 2nd British Infantry Division

THE VILLAGE

Naked kids with impish faces,
Coloured drinks and lemonade
Sugar-cane and ghee and onions
Stacked and stinking in the shade.
    Women shouting, screaming, touting
    Cursing, wagging heads and pouting
Getting quarter what they ask for
Grinning at the profit made.

Rows of pots and bowls and dishes,
Rice and spice and healing balms,
Pungent incense, reeking garlic
Bottles next a book of Psalms
    Sandals, matches, melons, latches,
    Coloured shirts with coloured patches
Rising grandly from the roof tops,
Lofty heads of swaying palms.

Solemn wide-eyed girls and infants
Clinging to their mother's hand,
Bearded ancients full of wisdom
Stand and talk, or merely stand
    Cowbells clattering, children yattering
    Startled bullocks snorting, scattering
Men who walk at noon are rightly
More than they can understand

Peter R. Carstairs[1]
2nd Reconnaissance Regiment
Taken from "*So This is India*"

---

1. Peter Carstairs was an officer in the 2nd Reconnaissance (6th Battalion, the Loyal Regiment (North Lancashire) of 2nd British Infantry Division. He produced a booklet of his impressions of India. The next five poems are from his book.

ON THE ROAD

Mile on mile of dusty roadway
Mostly bad and vile in parts,
Mile on mile of goaded bullocks
Pulling (oddly) bullock carts
    Lumbering long ones, lurching low ones,
    Swaying, sagging, down at heels ones,
No one cares a jot or tittle
When he travels, stops or starts

Raucous honks and klaxon braying
Cause the most unholy mess
Omnibus careering wildly
Labelled "Karnatak Express"
    Engine smoking, inmates poking
    Out their faces, gasping, choking
Our opinion most amusing
Trying for them none the less

Blinking through the gritty dust clouds,
Peering with discerning eyes,
Strange to say one finds that colour
In amongst the squalor lies
    Scarlet sheen or emerald green,
    Brilliant hues you've never seen
Silvery bangles, flowing saris
Fluttering shirt tails – blast these flies!

THE JUNGLE

Ploughing through the maze of timber
Hands and arms and faces torn
Branches catching on equipment,
Every blasted bush a thorn,
    Cutting, hacking, lumber-jacking,
    Compass reading, veering, tacking,
Monkeys jeering in the tree tops
Grinning lips curled back in scorn

Sudden clearings by the rivers,
Trees deformed by floods and rains,
Paddy fields all lush luxuriant
Product of some human's pains.
    Farmers sowing, cattle lowing,
    Cool and shady water flowing,
Gurgling round the stepping stones
Receiving all the village drains!

On along the narrow highway
Blinded with the pinky dust
Bullocks plunging into ditches,
Drivers scowling with distrust.
    Bamboo thickets, trilling crickets,
    Lop-eared goats and kids with rickets
Through the gloom and the fuming bullocks
Contemplate us with disgust.

CAMP

Early to bed and early to rise
To a sonorous bugle call
Neat little piles of buckets and spades
With "FIRE" adorning them all
    Neat little shapes of boots and capes,
    Folded neatly to cover the tapes
And most essential point to note
Identical one and all

Schemes by day and schemes by night
Causing many a worried frown
Attacking for the thousandth time
The same imaginary town
    Umpires, wearing armbands, swearing
    Black is white – directors tearing
Out their hair as troops are sweating
Standing "to" and "down"

Back to camp with filthy faces
Clothes and weapons thick with dust
Welcome "char" and soap and water
    Soon remove the outer crust.
    Washing, rubbing, cleaning, scrubbing,
Oiling, filling up and "grubbing"
By the way, in rainy seasons
"Dust" please read as "rust"

TOWN

Glass and concrete, stainless steel,
Streamlined structures, straight and clean
Overhanging balconies
On ancient beams that twist and lean
    Cast iron posts and columns – ghosts
    Of Queen Victoria's days – and hosts
Of gharries of her time, and lordly
Mansions next to hovels mean

B.E.S.T[1] double decker's
Slick and polished as a pin
Ancient single decker tram cars
Kicking up a fiendish din,
    Grating, banging crashing, clanging,
    Drivers ringing bells, haranguing
Swarms of overloaded cyclists
Deftly weaving out and in

Old and new all intermingle,
East and west all coincide
Carry on while pencils scribble
Morning, noon and eventide
    Colours noted, laughter quoted
    Note books soon replete devoted
To the fun and games around you
If your eyes are opened wide.

1. Local Bus Company.

THE PROVINCIAL TOWN

Police direct unheeding traffic
Cheery youngsters loudly suck
Lollipops, and fortune tellers
Ask the dupes to try their luck
  Merchants (seated) hold their heated
  Arguments with oft repeated
Waggings of their flowing beards
As bargains are arranged and struck

Beggars clutch with skinny fingers
Whining in a monotone
Students congregate at corners,
Fakirs sit and pray alone
  Tongas ringing, bouncing, bringing
  Screaming drivers – weird singing
To the noise of drums and cymbals
Screeching from a gramophone

Soldiers, usually black and grimy
"dobied"[1] to the finger tips
Spotless "whites" and "blues" and bush shirts
Dusky beauty, swaying hips
  Flowing locks and cotton frocks,
  Painted toe nails, dainty socks,
Cafes jammed with true bred Britons
Doubtless eating eggs and chips!

Peter R. Carstairs
2nd Reconnaissance Regiment
Taken from "*So This is India*"

1. **Dhobi** (English: "washerman") is a caste group of India. Their traditional occupation was washing clothes, i.e. laundry. The word dhobi is derived from the Hindi word dhona, which means to wash. (Wikipedia) Therefore, to do your dhobie - do your laundry; to be dobied – washed.

DIVE IN BROTHER

Nice and deep and not too wide
Easy to jump in quick
Those are the rules for a slit trench
See that you learn them quick

None of your sand bagged fancies
You haven't the time to spare
But plain as the spade that made them
Simple and starkly bare

We've dug them in sand on the seashore
(I thought my back would break)
We've dabbled with gypsum and granite
(my heart had the biggest ache)

We've savoured the joys of a nice firm clay
And there we ran nearest to form
But that was turned to a drainage scheme
To salvage our tent in a storm!

We've never had one you could really call home
Though we gave them our labour and love
But we often have guests at our little "At Home"
When things aren't too rosy above

We've even had Colonels and Generals
Drop in to pay us a call
For a Slit Trench's no Mansion or Palace
But it's useful when things start to fall

Anon
Taken from *Keynotes* – November 1943

OUR ANE[1] FOLK

In the midst of all the fighting, and the talking, reading, writing,
There's a saying comes to mind that's old and true;
And with all our battles glorious, and our armies so victorious
We should remember to give credit where its due

We are grateful to the Yanks for their heavy tanks
And their bombers, some the finest ever flown
We applaud the Russians too, our proved allies firm and true
But let us see to it we don't forget our own.

We have fighting French, and such men
Czechs, poles and Greeks and Dutchmen
And others exiled from their native shore
But we're bankrupt of our praise and all laudatory phrase,

Let us think of our own lads a little more.
And the Empire's countless legions from the world's most far
flung regions
Who straight away answered Freedom's clarion call;
They have added lasting fame to the Commonwealths proud
name, and still we are the bravest of them all.

So wherever they may roam, yet remember folks at home,
OUR LADS in all your prayers and hopes and fears;
For wherever they may fight, and they will do so with all their
might,
Though their lot be blood and toil and tears

J. H. M.
Taken from *Keynotes*

1. Jockanese (Scottish) means 'own'.

ANOPHELES'[1] LAMENT

The mozzies round my net each night
Sing tearfully their sad refrain

That it is easy to get in
But once they're in the must remain

For, as you know, their tiny tums,
Soon swell when they have staked their claim

And little holes that let them in
Would never let them out again

L.A.W.
A Soldier of the 2nd British Infantry Division
Taken from *Keynotes*
Also published in *Laugh With SEAC*

1. Anopheles mosquitoes still kill about 440,000 people each year because of malaria (Wikipedia) Until the introduction of the drug Mepacrine, the Allied Forces suffered around 120 casualties from the Anopheles' mosquito for every casualty from the Japanese.

ANOPHELES MINIMUS

Thou wretched plague, thou saboteur, thou pest,
Thou vile infester of each stagnant place,

Thou ruthless interferer with my rest,
Thou savage biter of my hands and face.

Thou trespasser within my sacred net,
Thou rude disturber of my peaceful dream

I'll be revenged on thee, I'll get thee yet –
To arms! To legs! apply the Mozzie cream

FROLIK

Taken from *Laugh With SEAC*

NOSTALGIA

There was a time – seems long ago
We cursed the ice, the sleet, the snow,
The raw, dank mists and pea soup fogs
And rain that pelted cats and dogs

Unhonoured then went spring: unseen
How grey gave way to fresher green
Then summer came – and went. Alas
How unperceived did autumn pass

Time marches on.....O woe! O Sorrow!
Its sun today and sun tomorrow
It's always fine – its fine today
Fine next week and yesterday.

We're brown as berries, tanned as leather,
With such loads of perfect weather,
Who bothers now to pause and say
"Good Morning. What a lovely day"

Or will we sigh for light and heat
When we are back in civvy street
And shiv'ring in our native land
Long for India's coral strand?

Anon
A Soldier of the 2nd British Infantry Division
Taken from *Keynotes*

AFTER TIFFIN

Once more it's here, that midday sun
And the hours when on Pelang we lie,
The hours when nothing can be done,
Time becomes eternity

Like an evil god of by-gone days,
Red visage, malevolent fury
Sentencing our hot minds to maze
We have no jury

How far are the fields of verdant green,
Our homes and the clement weather?
Are they only might have beens
Land of Never – Never?

In this land of heat and haze
Where all is dead or dying
To hold us captive all our days?
For time is flying

Yet when self-pity's voice is loudest
Think of those lost in the fray
Composed of England's best and proudest,
Dead are they!

They died that we with all our strength
With grim and great endeavour,
May, even at great cost or length
Free the world forever

Anon
A Soldier of the 2nd British Infantry Division
Taken from *Keynotes* – May 1943

FRAGRANT MINUTE

Now we're used to
India's smells

It makes me think
That when we're back

We shall find
That there, by contrast,

Even England
Smells quite strange

Anon
A soldier of the 2nd British Infantry Division
Taken from *Keynotes* – June 1943

ODE TO A SAUSAGE[1]

"It's sausages, What! Not again,
When will the stocks begin to wane?
Of sausages that should be pink,
Alas! Not so the Soya Link

A dark brown colour it emerges,
Oh, most sorrowful of dirges,
The cry goes up, what do you think,
For breakfast, it's the Soya Link.

When in the field what did we live on?
Not caviar or even pigeon
Nor wild duck of salmon pink
No! just the common Soya Link

So varied are its many uses,
That bean which USA produces
From plasticine for filling chinks
To explosives and Soya Links

The meat content is far from high
Whilst making it as pig passed by
And so said one "Ha Ha, methinks,
I'll call them Pork and Soya Links

---

1. The service men and women of South East Asia Command suffered from a lack of many things, such as clothing, food, ammunition and equipment. One of the things that many of them wished they had a shortage of was the sausage substitute – "**The Soya Link**".

Enough of this, let us not grumble,
When to the Dining Tent we stumble
Nor let our stomachs cowardly shrink
From bread and dip and Soya Link

Now bacon is another matter
Let's have some more and so grow fatter

Cpl /??/
A Soldier of the 2nd British Infantry Division
Taken from *Keynotes* – October 1943

THE LINK[1] WITH A PAST

Unwelcome link reposing on my plate
I frown on you but can abuse you not!

Eventual mastication is your fate,
Complete oblivion is your final lot

But from this weary world you do not pass
Without some wag has used your name in jest,

Some funster made of you a national farce
Some doggerel rhymester did his level best

To win a laugh from hungry fellows who
though rocked with mirth, consume you in the end

Which leads me to believe, when all is through
The final laugh is not on YOU my friend

FROLIK

Laugh With SEAC

1. The Soya Link – Sausage substitute.

ODE TO THE R.A.S.C[1]

Along the roads of India
The bullock convoys go
On the dusty roads of India
Patient and plodding and slow

The pace of the bullock is steadfast
By time he has never been vexed
If he fails to arrive on the right day
The next one will do – or the next.

On the busy roads of England
The convoys throng and muster
Through leafy lanes in England
The Bedford's hoot and bluster

The Bedford on duty is time bound
His schedule is fixed from above
But he's willing and fast and he makes it
With quite a bit of work on the gov.

There's a feud 'twixt the Bull and the Bedford
Thrown together by unhappy fate,
One gentle and timeless and sedate
One tied to the hour and the date

The bullock remains contemplative
The Bedford has got to get there
So they clash every day on the highways
And both feel it's rather unfair

---

1. Royal Army Service Corps.

The Bedford's a stranger intruding
And strangers are apt to be rough
The Bullocks been here slightly longer,
And feels that he ought to get tough

East is East and West is West
But sometimes the twain must meet
When this happens, just pause and consider
A bullock in Oxford Street?

Anon
Taken from *Keynotes* – March 1943

G 1098[1] AND ALL THAT

It started in England long years ago,
It's a typical Army tale of woe.
Just lend your ears to our hymn of hate
As we tell the tale of G 1098.

We packed it in crates and bound it with rope,
Hurrah, it is finished; such was our hope.
"That's just where you're wrong," the serjeant did state,
"We've to check it again, this G 1098.

We stared in amazement and felt ourselves sway,
we'd only just put the damned stuff away.
"Today's a holiday...we've got a date."
"That's true," said the serj. "With the G 1098."

At that old Micky turned scarlet with ire,
And out of his nostrils came dragon like fire,
"They've made an advance in the west – so they state.
And the job for today is G 1098."

There were picks and shovels, buckets and pails,
Hammers and tenons, and plenty of nails.
But this much is certain, sure as fate,
There'll be something gone in the G 1098.

---

1. The G 1098 or to give it the full title – Army Form General 1098 – is the complete list of equipment held by a unit, be it a Company, a Battalion or a Brigade. It lists everything from an Abacus (if held on the G 1098!) to a xylophone, (also if held on the G 1098) that the particular unit is entitled to hold. There is a peacetime holding and a wartime holding, and there is no denying it or claiming that you never had it – if it is on your G 1098!!

The NCO'S faces were full of lament,
As they waited in gloom outside the QM's tent
A whistle is lost and sad is your fate,
If it isn't returned to the G 1098.

We've played with toggles and wallowed in mud,
We've swum in the ocean and trickled with blood.
Then its back again to our usual fate,
Of packing and checking the G 1098

There's many a slip twixt the cup and the lip,
There's many are lured by the swing of a hip,
But the deadliest weapon that man did create
Is that blankety blankety G 1098.

As into the battle we proudly advance,
And we know that the enemy hasn't a chance
For our role is that we patiently wait,
For the signal to check the G 1098

The Gatling's jammed and the Colonel's dead,
The captains down with the wound in the head,
Comes the clarion call we all await –
"Go to it lads, check the G 1098."

There's a breathless hush in the camp tonight,
The serjeant's fallen and died of fright,
Someone has blundered – sad to relate –
in painting the signs of G 1098

The original lines of the poem can be found
On priceless parchment in bundles bound,
Five sheets per day is the army rate –
This was filched from the G 1098

There's a moral to this humble poem,
Which should be hung in every home,
This war will be won – soon or late,
By the constant checking of the G 1098.

Anon
A Soldier of the 2nd British Infantry Division
Taken from *Keynotes* – April 1943

REMEMBER ME

When the battery's flat and the car will not start,
Or the Bandix doesn't run free,
If the gear lever grates, or the diff vibrates, –
They remember the R.E.M.E.[1]

If a watch does not tick, or the spring's lost its kick,
Or the compasses do not agree,
If a speedo is reading the miles off too quick, -
They remember the R.E.M.E.

Should they need Alloy Flux, or instruction books,
Or simply a duplicate key,
They seems to forget that the stuff's hard to get,
And come scrounge from the R.E.M.E!

When the 'piece'[2] won't run out, or a sights had a clout,
Or their laying is out a degree,
If the recoil is excessive, Its really impressive
How they shout for R.E.M.E.

---

1 Royal Electrical and Mechanical Engineers. Prior to WW2, the repair and maintenance of equipment and machinery was largely the responsibility of the Corps that used it. However, during WW2, the increase in quantity and complexity of the equipment exposed the flaws in this system. Pursuant to the recommendation of a Committee on Skilled Men in the Services, the Corps of Royal Electrical and Mechanical Engineers was formed on 1 October 1942.

2. Artillery piece – the gun.

When they hand out their praises in sweet honeyed phrases,
On the day that we achieve victory,
It would please us a lot if the bigwigs did not
FORGET THE R.E.M.E

Anon
A Soldier of the 2nd British Infantry Division
Taken from *Keynotes* – April 1943

EPIC OF A GLUTTON

We went to France for Battle, but we had to cool our heels
So we spent our time in tasting wine and flirting with "les filles"
We learned a lot, those blissful days – our tastes developed fast
Till the gods above cried "Havoc" and we put aside the past
For we slaked our thirst with water and forgot the wine and beer
And hundred foreign dishes our palates found so dear.

We landed back with thankful hearts and aching in our guts
And solaced them with penny buns and tea in NAAFI huts
We stooged around a rationed land although we couldn't grumble
Of what we had was plenty albeit it was humble

Then they broke it gently, we were for the mystic East
We thought of what we'd oftimes read and girdled for the feast
Alas! That we were not warned, by some timely benefactor
Of char and Wads as handed out by a dusky hued contractor
Oh Mist Bicarb Oh Sodi Bic for ever hear my plea
And help to fortify my guts against the cursed Ghi!

Enough of all these foreign lands, these dishes fine and rare,
There's tripe and onions back at home; God grant, I'll soon be there.

WO2 Kenneth Norman Marwood
6th Field Ambulance
Royal Army Medical Corps
2nd British Infantry Division

GRUB STAKES

I like a high-class dinner
Especially served in state
With spotless shining silver
And expensive Chinese plate

I like a snack in Soho
Where the food's beyond compare
Where nothing's too expensive
And every dish is rare

I like a Chinese restaurant
As famed throughout the east
Where Rupees five will foot the bill
For quite a lengthy feast

I like my bread and cheese and beer
In an ancient English pub
I like my light refreshment[1]
In an Indian Coffee Club

---

1. Light Refreshment is still the term used in India today. Whilst in the UK, we would be likely to say, "would you like a cup of coffee", in India – it's "would you care for some light refreshment".

But, until I joined the Army
I never savoured fully
The joys of Mess Tin cooking
With spuds and beans and bully[2]

Gone are the days when I toyed with food
When the glare and the glitter came first
For I know what it's like to be hungry
And I know what it's like to thirst!

Submitted *by N. M. in 1943*
A Soldier of the 2nd British Infantry Division
Taken from *Keynotes*

---

2. Bully – Bully Beef, also known as **Corned Beef** is a salt-cured beef product, usually sold in tins. The term comes from the treatment of the meat with large grained rock salt, also called "corns" of salt. It is featured as an ingredient in many cuisines (Wikipedia). Because of the temperatures in India & Burma, the contents of the tin were capable of being poured out, rather than being removed as a single lump ready for slicing.

THE TERRIBLE TALE OF A CHRISTMAS PUD

Come listen to me and I'll tell you
A terrible tale of the east
How a man with size twelve Cossacks
Mucked up a Christmas feast

The battery had 'Come to action'
On this ill-fated night
And dinner had to be dished out
With ne'er a glimmer of light

The food was in the dixies
In a row along the ground
The cooks had started 'lobbing up'
The queue wound slowly round

Twelve months these men had waited
And now they felt so chuffed
Their eyes shone in the darkness
At the thought of Christmas Duff

Not a sound was heard
Not a mess tin clashed
When the silence was suddenly riven
By a strangled cry
That went up to the sky
"He's stood in the Christmas Pudden"

He was known as "Erotic Edna"
To the boys in the Burma sphere
Though why he was called 'Erotic'
Never was very clear

There he stood in the Christmas Pudden
His face was red with shame
He said "now lads, my eyes are bad,
I can't take all the blame"

As they silently stood
And gazed at the food
Their hope all dashed to pieces
Came an angry cry, blame my eye
Thank God he's the last of the species

As he withdrew, the air was blue
The lads had had enough
"Alas!" they said, "it looks as if
We've had our Christmas Duff"

Then someone sprang to the rescue
With knife and fingers too
They scrapped off enough of the mess
To serve all but a few

Then as they all sat eating
Came a cry from one galoot
"Here Sir, is one of your heel plates
Stick it back on your daisy root"

It was Christmas night in Burma,
But the lads stuck up their snoots
"We don't want your Christmas pudding
Stick it back on Edna's boots"

Now all you Orderly Officers
Let this be a lesson to you
If you've got to stand in something
For God's sake stand in the stew!

Attributed to Jock Campbell
16th Field Regiment Royal Artillary

CHRISTMAS REMEMBRANCE

It is not framed in costly gold
Nor does it hang where all may see
But in its hiding place I hold
Your ever-precious memory
And though we are so far apart
I keep it framed dear,
In my heart

Sgt Frank 'Dago' Davis
16th Field Regiment Royal Artillery
2nd British Infantry Division

In a Christmas greeting to his wife, India 1943

PART 4 – ARAKAN 1944

The game had changed by this stage. There had been a whole raft of changes to the British /Indian Army, not just in the command structure but also in the tactics used to combat the expertise of the Japanese. No longer was there to be a withdrawal when confronted by the Japanese. The British & Indian forces were to form their own defensive boxes and to stand fast in the face of an attack. Where they stood is where they would fight and where they would be re-supplied. Each command and sub unit was to be responsible for its own defence. Operations were to continue throughout the monsoon rather than to scale down as had been the practice previously.

The South East Asia Command (SEAC) had been created with Rear Admiral, Lord Louis Mountbatten in Command. The 14th Army had been formed from the old Eastern Army and Lieutenant General William Slim placed in command of it. He had put into practice the lessons learned from the retreat from Burma in 1942 and from the Arakan in 1943. As a result the 14th Army was tougher, leaner and more confident of its ability to defeat the Japanese. The infrastructure was now in place to allow the rapid deployment of troops across the battlefield and the preparations for a limited incursion into Burma had commenced.

XV Corps in the Arakan were also to push forward but the Japanese 'Operation C' pre-empted this and so began the Second Arakan Campaign. The results this time were quite different with the Allied forces standing fast, forcing the Japanese to batter themselves against prepared defensive positions. This move by the Japanese developed into Operation

U-GO with the invasion of India by the Japanese 15th Army under Lieutenant General Renya Mutaguchi, who sent his 31st Division under Lieutenant General Kotoku Sato across the hills to fall on Kohima.

These changes to the tactics and command structure were to highlight the deficiencies in the Japanese system of command. Slim placed logistics and morale at the head of his list to prepare for decisive battle. The Japanese relied on past practice and experience in which they captured what they needed from the retreating British. Mutaguchi equipped his men with 3 weeks supply of food and all the ammunition they could carry.

However, this time the British did not withdraw. This time they denied access to stores and equipment and the Japanese soon began to run out of everything they needed.

Even at this late point, Mutaguchi could have altered his logistic plans. But Slim's planned withdrawal of his Divisions to the Imphal Plain convinced Mutaguchi that his plan was working and the British were yet again falling back as they had done each time he had encountered them. Instead Slim was drawing the Japanese Imperial Forces onto ground of his own choosing and shortening his supply line and lengthening those of the Japanese. The withdrawal onto the Imphal Plain meant also that Slim could use his armour in numbers rather in small packets. This did not bode well for the Japanese!

JUNGLE FASHIONS

"... The Japanese broke into a Headquarters and the Colonel, not having time to change, had to fight in his pyjamas till four o'clock..." (Daily Paper)

The enemy forgot to knock,
The Colonel[1] got a nasty shock,
And had to fight till 4 o'clock
    In his pyjamas:

No doubt the strangest sight in war,
The like we haven't seen before,
It mustn't happen any more,
    These things alarm us

Imagine A.T.S.[2] in scanties,
Manning their A.A.[3] gun in panties,
And clad in glittering diamantes
    Perhaps 'twould charm us

It's nice to undress, when it's hot,
But Colonels, No! most certainly not,
How horrible if he'd been shot
    In his pyjamas

---

1. The 'Colonel' referred to is actually Major General Frank Messervy, General Officer Commanding 7th Indian Infantry Division who was surprised by the Japanese at Laung Chaung in the Arakan.

2. Auxiliary Territorial Services – Forerunner of the Woman's Royal Army Corps.

3. Anti-Aircraft.

In jungle fighting it's not right
To go to bed by candle light,
Nor dress for dinner every night –
   These things would harm us;

But still it is a solemn thought
That when a battle's being fought,
the Colonel might be getting caught
   In his pyjamas

Just wait till Winston[4] hears the news,
His Sunday best he must refuse,
And give the House his latest views
   IN HIS PYJAMAS.

Lance Corporal McLelland
Taken from *Keynotes*

4. Winston Churchill – The wartime British Prime Minister.

DIVE BOMBER

I'm Minnie, the mad mosquito
You've heard of me, I'll bet
I hang around the bunks at night
To see what I can get

My legs are long and shapely
The boys admire my knees
They gaze upon my torso
For I really am a tease

My drone is like the Stuka
I've heard the sentries say
I like to make them dizzy
And turn the blighters grey

Oh how they try to swat me
They sweat and how they swear
They've even tried the butt stroke
But Minnies never there

Oh the Red Caps, how they love me
That's where the squaddy grieves
For when he wanders out at nights
It's "Drop those ruddy sleeves"[1]

---

1. In order to reduce the high incidence of malaria, Slim issued orders that there was to be no open-air bathing, no shorts or short sleeves after 1800 hours – it worked!

I'm Minnie, the mad mosquito
I live in swamp and sluice
I fly around the nets at night
In search of human juice

And when I bite, I cackle
I suck in lovely blood
And then I go and settle
On lovely chinks of mud

I nestle in the sunshine
My lovely eggs I lay
They'll all be little 'Minnies'
To help me out some day

So, be careful lest I bite you
When you are on a scheme
I'm Minnie the mad mosquito
And I thrive on 'Mozzy cream'

JHM
A Soldier of the 2nd British Infantry Division
Taken from *Keynotes* – March 1944

TIME

Time is just a tiny word
A word with so much meaning
Something that can heal the heart
When all the world lies bleeding

Tiresome days are hard to take
The nights are long and weary
Loved ones all we now forsake
For this thing men call Glory

Time alone will heal the wound
The war between the nations
Time alone will mend the heart
And help our new creations

Time alone will see us through
The dark drear days of sadness
Make our wishes all come true
And fill our hearts with gladness

Cpl G Bridges
A Soldier of the 2nd British Infantry Division
Taken from *Keynotes* – March 1944

SO SORRY CHAPS

Who hasn't, since he first became
Possessed of Number, Rank AND Name
Experienced all the fuss and tantrums
When the news o'er placid camp runs,
"The General's coming!"

Whilst being served with breakfast fare,
Above your head (without much care),
A bloke starts splashing white-wash round
As though he hopes that he'll confound
The General – when he comes.

The cookhouse Wallahs, clad in white,
Discard their 'Field Grey' (ghastly sight),
And highly polish countless pails,
Whilst e'en the cook's rake out their nails,
As the General's coming.

The menu that's laid on is – well,
T'would not be amiss in the 'Taj' Hotel,
Makes lads lined up in the cookhouse queue,
Saying, "Blimey, what's happened – no bully stew?"
No – the General's coming

The bugler whom the Fates decreed
Shall sound the Welcome on his reed,
Then causes untold consternation – blows the General
    Salutation,
For a simple chap who's come, to fix some faulty sanitation
And the General's still not come.

When all the camp is nigh in tears,
Amidst a grinding clash of gears,
Comes a message – borne by Don R[1],
Signed by "White Cliffs" (General Dover)[2],
Saying "Sorry, cannot make it – Maybe pop along tomorrow

N.J.
A Soldier of the 2nd British Infantry Division
Taken from *Keynotes* – March 1944

---

1. Don R – Dispatch Rider.

2. This may refer to Major General John Grover, the General Officer Commanding, 2nd British Infantry Division. Known (behind his back) as 'Black Jack', this may be a play on words to protect the author – whoever he might be!

ARAKAN PATROL

Beside a dusty road on the Arakan
A Japanese sniper dies
His cherry blossom far away
There's nothing here but flies

In blazing sun, we had spread out flat
To listen to his Rat, Tat, Tat,
Beneath a tree, a blowout hole
His bloody body stank,
Thought no man could reach him there
He forgot about the tank

Our tank, it moved back through the canes
Between us and the japs
To see us safely home again
So we could take a nap

Private Raymond Street
Company runner
4th Battalion, Queens Own Royal West Kent Regiment
(4 RWK)[1]

1. 4 RWK was in 161 Indian Infantry Brigade, of 5th Indian Infantry Division. They were airlifted from the Arakan in time to stand against the Japanese 31st Division at the Siege of Kohima. The 5th Indian Infantry Division was one of the few Allied formations to have fought the Germans, the Italians and the Japanese.

ALL RIGHT LADS

Alright lads take him back
Down along that muddy track
Move it lads, the sergeant said,
Move it lads and help young Fred
Hot blue skies, hawk and kites
Not much like the Isle of Wight.

Alright lads, shells incoming
Watch it Bill, the mules are running
Shrapnel hits the Mango tree
Auntie Flo has come to tea

Alright lads let’s tend his wound,
Mother just arrived from Broome
Smoke is coming from the funnel
It’s getting dark, we’re in a tunnel

Alright lads let’s leave him be
It’s a wicked world
He’s all at sea.

Private Raymond Street
Company runner
4th Battalion, Queens Own Royal West Kent Regiment
(4 RWK)

PART 5 – KOHIMA

THE BATTLEGROUND

When the men of the 2nd British Infantry Division first saw the little hill town of Kohima, it was already a war shattered shell of a place set in a scarred countryside where the earth was torn and the trees blasted and twisted by high explosive. To this desolate scene, 2nd British Infantry Division added its own quota of destruction. Its artillery, its tanks, its mortars and the Royal Engineers with their demolition charges, poured on to the Japanese positions around Kohima a hail of metal and explosives which turned the ridges where it fell into chaos.

Then came the infantry, storming the bunkers day after day. The barrage had done its work well, but it could not destroy all the enemy machine guns, all the enemy mortars, or all of their fox holes with their riflemen and grenadiers. The Divisional infantry, suffering heavy losses, eventually succeeded in pushing the Japanese forces from Naga Village, Aradura Spur and the Kohima Ridge and forcing them into retreat down the Imphal Road.

But there were many hundreds of men who lay quietly in rough graves along the hills and ridges they had won. They were men from Scotland and from Wales, from East Anglia, and from the North Country round Durham and Manchester, from the West Country, Berkshire and Buckinghamshire. With them lay men of the tanks, gunners, sappers and signals who had also played such a major part in this terrible battle.

Seventy-five years later, the destroyed buildings have been replaced and added to. The quick lush growth of Nagaland has covered the scarred earth and the trees are all renewed although some of the older trees still bear witness to the Battle through healed bullet holes and shrapnel scars. There is little left now to tell the visitor of the struggle which went on in the summer of 1944. However, the men of the 2nd British Infantry Division were not willing that their comrades who had fallen, should be so easily forgotten. They gathered their dead together in groups of graves, marked each with its own white cross and placed them on a site below where the District Commissioner's Bungalow had stood. This was where much of the hardest fighting took place and here today stands the 2nd British Infantry Division's Memorial to those who were lost from its ranks. The Memorial was designed and built by men of the Division, and the expense of its stone and copper was borne by men of every unit which came down the road from Dimapur with Major General John Grover to meet the Japanese in the early days of April 1944. It is the product of men's will to recognise with the unstinting use of their own skill and labour and their own resources the human worth of those who fought beside them.

The principal feature of the 2nd British Infantry Division's Memorial is the great monolith that was brought from the hills and placed in position by 200 of the local Naga tribesmen, who would accept no payment for their work. Behind this massive pillar runs a semi-circular wall of grey dressed stone, engraved with the Battle's Roll of Honour. This wall is carried on into the wings on both sides and the whole is paved with stone and approached by a pleasing sweep of shallow semi-circular steps.

Today the Memorial stands above the sharp bend in the Dimapur/Imphal road looking towards Naga Village and the tracks and hills beyond. Behind the memorial, stretching back up the steep slope lie the neat rows of graves of the British and Indian soldiers, and beyond this where the District Commissioner's bungalow once stood, with the famous tennis court alongside it stands another Memorial, this one to the Hindu and Muslim soldiers who also fell at the Battle.

From this now peaceful setting can be seen the slopes of Aradura and that part of the ridge, where men of the Royal Scots and the Royal Norfolk Regiment emerged from the jungle to take the Japanese in the rear. To the north and below lies Hospital Spur, scene of some of the earliest fighting and perhaps the sorest trial of all for the men who held it.

The memorial is thus the fitting tribute of a proud formation to their friends who with them showed, as their Army Commander told them, "what first class British troops can do at their very best". It is also a tribute – a promise – by those who did go home, that they would not forget to speak of those who stayed behind, nor to of tell how they forsook the daylight in order that so many more might live in hope and freedom from fear.

This then, is the memorial to the men of the 2nd British Infantry Division who fell in what was one of the most brutal and vicious battles of the whole war. Men who conformed to Field Marshal Sir William Slim's definition of courage, when he said in his book[1] on the subject:

1. *Courage – And Other Broadcasts.*

"While nations vary in the amount of their courage, they vary too in its type. We, the British, have our own special kind of courage, the courage that goes on – and endurance is the very essence of courage. Courage is a long–term virtue. Anyone can be brave for a little while. The British are no braver than the Germans, the French, the Italians or anybody else, but they are brave for a bit longer. This going on being brave when most others would have given up has been a racial characteristic of our courage."

It stands at the foot of Garrison Hill and has a plate of bronze affixed to the monolith of Naga stone. On that plate is inscribed the Kohima Epitaph, a translation of an old Greek epigram spoken by Simonides to honour the Spartans who fell at the Battle of Thermopylae in 480 BC and which reads thus.

When you go home
Tell them of us and say,
For your tomorrow
We gave our today

In recent years, the epitaph has been used on an increasing number of occasions to commemorate the lives of members of British forces killed in both World Wars and in other military actions. Yet despite the fact that these words are now so widely known, their association with the 2nd British Infantry Division appears not to be, which is perhaps in keeping with the notion of a Forgotten Army fighting a Forgotten War. What remains important however, is that it had its genesis in the aftermath of a battle that marked one of the most significant turning points in the whole of the Second World War.

PERICLES FUNERAL ORATION

The Oration was given by Pericles, the Athenian Leader after the Battle of Samos in the Peloponnesian Wars, circa 430 BC. It is included in this book because it reflects closely the circumstances encountered by British & Indian Forces at the Siege of Kohima It is also read out at each Kohima Memorial Day service.

> "Let your thoughts dwell day by day on your country's true greatness and when you realise her grandeur, remember it is a heritage won for you by dauntless men who knew their duty and did it.
>
> In the hour of trial, the one thing they feared was dishonour.
>
> They failed not their motherland but laid their gallant lives at her feet.
>
> In one great host did they give themselves to death but each one, man by man, has won imperishable praise.
>
> Each one has won a glorious grave – not the sepulchre of earth wherein they lie but the everlasting tomb of Remembrance that will live on the lips, that will blossom on the deeds of their Countrymen the world over.
>
> For the whole world is the sepulchre of heroes.
>
> Monuments may rise, and tablets be set up to them in their own land, but on the far-off shores, there is an abiding memorial that no pen or chisel has raised.
>
> It is graven, not on stone or brass – but on the living heart of humanity.
>
> Take these men for your example, like them remember that prosperity and true happiness can only be for the free and that freedom is the possession of those alone who have the courage to defend it."

NO TEARS WERE SHED AT KOHIMA

We were the ones who brought you grief
We died in a battle that was beyond belief
We were the ones who bore the pain
And we were buried in the monsoon rain
"No tears were shed at Kohima"

Our bodies are buried, but we are not there
We are the raindrops in the midnight air
We are the weather so warm and fair
We are the breeze that rustles your hair
"No tears were shed at Kohima"

We are the stars in the midnight skies
The Christmas delight in a small child's eyes
We are the pillows where you lay your head
We are the vision at the foot of your bed
"No tears were shed at Kohima"

You could not go to see our graves
The resting place of the young and brave
It will not be safe they always say
Yet because of the likes of us
They enjoy their freedom today
"No tears were shed at Kohima"

Fusilier John Done
1st/8th Battalion, Lancashire Fusiliers
Attached to 143 Special Service Company[1]
Headquarters 2nd British Infantry Division

1. The Special Service Company had men from every regiment within the Division. They were troops who were used as a Quick

Reaction Force (QRF) and could be quickly sent to bolster an area of the battlefield that was in difficulties. They could also be used as a special task force. Other formations within the Indian Army had similar Special Service Companies.

The poem above is recited each year at the Kohima Memorial Day in York.

John Done has written several poems which are included here. The next four poems are his work.

IF ONLY

If only we could meet again
If only for a day
We would have a thousand things to do
A million words to say
We would talk about the things we had
That times that we were happy
The times that we were sad
If only we could meet again
If only for a day

If only we could meet again
If only in a dream
You know the world forgot about us
As we fought in the monsoon rain
I saw the horror on your face
When your body felt the pain
I held your hand so gently
As you slowly passed away

If only we could meet again
If only for a while
Then I'd see your cheeky grin
Your wonderful laughing smile
We stood when you were buried
On that monsoon, rainy day
There is one thing I would tell you
Through your suffering and pain
Because the things you fought and died for
You laid down your life in vain.

A RIVER OF TEARS

The battle you were killed in was horrific
It confirmed all of my fears
When we both said goodbye
With a wave and a sigh
Since then, I've cried me a river of tears

Here comes the night
I'll be lonely wishing you ever near
I know you are there to answer my prayer
Till then
I'll cry me a river of tears

I turn to my heart when I'm lonely
In my dreams, you'll always be there
You touch my hand, a moment we share
And then
I'll cry me a river of tears

I can't stand at your graveside and mourn you
You are buried so far away
You are still on my mind all through the years
And I've
Cried me a river of tears

NOT JUST ORDINARY MEN

A million men fought in Burma
All young boys had to go
Some of them were sent to Kohima
To fight a sadistic foe
They gave them a bush hat and a rifle
The time! We'll tell you when
And when you've done all your fighting
You'll not be ordinary men

You had to survive in the jungle
And life was not very good
You caught all kinds of diseases
And the leeches were sucking your blood
You went without food and water
The monsoon was not very kind
But things like that didn't stop you
You had a lot more things on your mind
The fighting lasted for hours you soon realise then
But you keep on killing and fighting
Because you are not just ordinary men

Thousands were killed in action
They are laid peacefully to rest on a hillside at Kohima
Where God accepted only the best
The rest of you went home to your loved ones
Of you there were many kinds
With your broken and mangled bodies
And your mentally disturbed minds
When you sit at rest in your armchair
And your thoughts wander here and there
You remember that you fought with an army
Of not just ordinary men

The people of this land will forget you
Of that there can be no doubt
When you try to tell them your story you will realise
Very soon that the way people accept you
Kohima could well have been on the moon
After a very long time, say after fifty years
They will decide to listen to your story
So that everyone will hear
They will hear of your pain and suffering
And maybe they will begin to realise then
That the forgotten men of Kohima
Were not just ordinary men.

REFLECTIONS FROM KOHIMA 1944

Don't stand and weep for me
I am the wind
I'm wild and free
I am the mist in the cold night air
I am the summertime warm and fair
I am the gentle autumn rain
I am the sun on the ripened grain
I'll be there when you lie in your bed
I am the pillow where you lay your head
In a raging storm, I am the eye
I am a thousand birds that fly
Don't stand and weep for me
I am the wind
I'm wild and free
Remember every word of love that I said
I am the vision at the foot of your bed
I am the stars that shine in the night
A beautiful eagle in the morning light
Don't stand and weep for me
I am the wind
I'm wild and free

Fusilier John Done
1st/8th Battalion, Lancashire Fusiliers
Attached to 143 Special Service Company
Headquarters 2nd British Infantry Division

SIEGE OF KOHIMA – APRIL 1944

3000 men stand to at dawn
20,000 Nippon to meet, this sunny morn,
It's Easter time, no eggs, no corn
Cicadas screech and stop
Outmatched by screaming shells
I burrow deep and throw earth on top

So, this is me, no flags or cheers
To stop a Nippon charge
Only bloody hell and slaughter
With a throat that craves for water
No cheery drinks or 'well done lads'
'Here, drink your fill'

We just reload our rifles
Thank goodness, this time
We held the hill[1]

'Crack-pop[2]' a Nippon rifle snipes
No muleteer, his bloody flank to wipe
A mule stands, quietly bleeding
Into a tiny heap of hay.
'Johnny get your gun', the Bren gun said
'To pass his day away[3]

---

1. Garrison Hill.
2. The distinctive sound of a Japanese rifle.
3. Presumably to put the mule out of its misery.

The ground we hold gets shorter,
Our wounded cry for water,
Orders – 'hold for 2 days more'
We make that two days, four
Before help begins to pour
Its water down our throats

The dead are all around
With eighty strong, we move along
To leave this shattered ground
Eighteen days have passed
All Heroes now, unwashed and tired
Thank God! this is the last[4]

Private Raymond Street[5]
4th Battalion, Queens Own Royal West Kent Regiment

Notes 4 and 5 below are personal notes attached by Private Street

4. It was not the last, we members of the 4 RWK, after a short two weeks or so of rest, moved back up outside Kohima again. Then moving in to clear the Jessami track in the Naga Hills of Japanese troops. We passed through Imphal to clear the Silchar track through the monsoon. Later the Chinn Hills, Tiddim, Kalewa and the Chocolate Staircase almost to the Chindwin river.

5. Out of about 450 men from 4 RWK who defended the town and hills, only about eighty of them walked off the hill at the end of the Siege. Some of them were wounded, our badly wounded had left earlier. I was one of the very few unwounded. The rest we left on the hill under a cross. They gave their todays for your tomorrows.

IN KOHIMA HILLS[1]

In the hills, they fought and died
So stubbornly instilled with matchless pride
With unfaltering stride, no matter the task
Victory they brought, and triumph unsurpassed

Now the silent tribute to victory gained
Stands a memorial, selflessly attained
Sleep on dear Comrades! Your glorious endeavour
Remains in our hearts, and all men's forever

And here they lie in deathless sleep
They gave their all, for freedom to keep
Embraced by the hills, who witnessed my story
Their tale will live forever in Glory

An epic of courage this poem reveals
Of those who fell in the Kohima Hills
And when you go home remember them: say
For your tomorrow, they gave their today

5728932 Private Humphrey Silkman[2]
2nd Battalion, The Dorsetshire Regiment
2nd British Infantry Division

Humphrey Silkman is remembered with honour in this publication

---

1. Because of the Kohima Epitaph in this poem, it is believed to have been written after the Dedication of the 2nd British Infantry Division Memorial in November 1944.

2. Died in the advance to Mandalay 10th March 1945. He is buried in Taukkyan War Cemetery. His grave reference is 18. F. 15.

5728932 PRIVATE
H. SILKMAN
THE DORSETSHIRE REGIMENT
10TH MARCH 1945 AGE 28
HE DIED THAT WE MIGHT LIVE IN PEACE.
WE REMEMBER - MOTHER AND FAMILY, LONDON

KOHIMA # 1

Tremble of leaf and bloom
Echoes the crash and boom
Sending them to their doom
The skies swift pleasure

Movement of hand and eye
Stillness of those who die
Softly the winds that lie
In ageless measure

Flash of a bright birds wing
Stab of a bullets sting
Killed by so small a thing?
This heart's rich treasure

Shadow and light and shade
Fall where their limbs are laid
Those who so dearly paid
To earn this leisure.

Gunner Richard George
99th (Royal Buckinghamshire Yeomanry) Field Regiment
Royal Artillery

KOHIMA # 2

It was down at a place called Kohima,
Where most of the fighting was done,
T'was there that a poor British tommy
Was shot by a Japanese gun.

As he lay on his elbow and dying
The blood from his wound did flow red,
He called his comrades around him
And these were the last words he said.

Bury me out in the jungle
Under the old Burmese sun
My duty for England is done

But when you go home to old blighty
And the war is all over and won,
Remember the poor British tommy
Buried under the old Burmese sun.

Anon
2nd British Infantry Division

KOHIMA #3

There's a place in the east called Kohima
Where the Japanese made their stand
Where the boys of the 2nd British Infantry Division
Fought a fight that won the hand

From Kohima on to Imphal
From Imphal to Tamu
From Imphal through Death Valley
And across the Chindwin too.

The Japs retreated to Yeha
With the Div. upon their tails
They were from dear old England
Scotland, Ireland and Wales

From Yeha they fought at Shwebo
From Shewbo onto Myamyo
Then across the Irrawaddy
And on to Mandalay

Anon

GARRISON HILL # 1

Come along old comrades
We've a story to spill
About all our mates and buddies
Who are buried on Garrison Hill
You know it's a grave yard
Filled with thousands of graves
With the bodies of all our soldiers
All so young and so brave

Early in the morning
When the weather is cool
The children lay beautiful flowers
On their way to school
When they have finished their lessons
They all walk down the lanes
They go back to grave yard
To talk to the soldiers again

We all know on Garrison that
There is no claim to fame
Because every grave stone
Is exactly the same
They're all in black marble
With their number, rank, and name
Where everyone is equal
And no one takes the blame

You know old comrades
It gives you no thrill
To remember the lads
Up there on Garrison Hill
When you think of the bad times
Your memories and thoughts you bare
It was only the luck of the Irish
We were not all buried up there.

Fusilier John Done
1st/8th Battalion Lancashire Fusiliers
Attached 143 Special Service Company
Headquarters 2nd British Infantry Division

GARRISON HILL #2

Lazily sailing in the breeze
The 'chutes came drifting down
To drape with silk the battered trees
That clothe the mountains crown

With anxious eyes, we watch their fate
How blows the wind today?"
God grant their course is true and straight –
We pray they drift our way

WO2 Kenneth Norman Marwood
6 Field Ambulance
Royal Army Medical Corps
2nd British Infantry Division

THE EVENING VIGIL

"Ten minutes to seven" – the word goes around
The sun starts to redden, alights on a mound
Of black cloud intruding on blue

In mud smothered clothes, men emerge from the ground
Stretch weary limbs with barely a sound
Then – quiet – for they're "Standing to"

With dusk, the sounds of the jungle abound
Cicadas and crickets – and some distant hound
Then – quiet – are they listening too?

Maurice J Franses – Kohima 1944
An officer in the 2nd Battalion the Royal Norfolk Regiment
2nd British Infantry Division

IN THE RISING SUN[1]

On this day let the bugle call
Past Memories of heroes all
Who rivers crossed and mountains climbed
To fight and to die and to leave behind
A small grey stone in the rising sun

Those who survive will remember one
Tall and brave and a Northern son[2]
Someone heard him, wounded, cry
"Now hear this message ere I die
My spirit will live in the rising sun"

Lieutenant Andrew Watson[3] GM
1st/8th Battalion Lancashire Fusiliers
2nd British Infantry Division

---

1. In memory of Fusilier Harold (Tiny) Henthorn 1st/8th Lancashire Fusiliers KIA 25 April 1944 – Kohima aged 27 years.
2. This poem was converted to a hymn for a Memorial Service for Harold Henthorne.
3. During this action Lt Watson himself was wounded. His lower left arm was almost completely severed by a bullet that entered at the wrist and travelled up to the elbow. Several operations and many years later, he regained limited use of his arm.

3453642 Fusilier Harold (Tiny) Henthorn is remembered here for his sacrifice

TO JOHN ROSTRON[1] DSO

Killed in Action 21 April 1944

They said you had gone but it didn't seem true
I couldn't believe it – it couldn't be you
With your eager mind
And your humour gay
And your heart so kind
And your friendly way
I thought of the things you were planning to do and I couldn't believe it
No Johnny – not you

And I didn't believe it was true, until
I saw the sun on a little green hill
And I thought of the downs that I knew far away
And remembering something I wanted to say
To you, because you'd know what I'd mean
And see exactly what I had seen
Something I wanted at once to share –
I turned to tell you – but you were not there
And then I knew that you had gone
And I was left to watch alone.

Reverend Kenneth W Parkhurst MBE HCF
Chaplain to 1st Battalion Royal Welsh Fusiliers –
2nd British Infantry Division

---

1. Captain John Norfolk Rostron DSO – 1st Battalion, Royal Welch Fusiliers was killed in action on 22nd April 1944 and is commemorated on the Rangoon Memorial. This would indicate that his remains were not identified.

KOHIMA 1944

I do not grieve for the men who fell at Kohima
They would disdain my tears
I saw the young men, trailing their arms
Move off to the position on the spur[1]
And a great grief seized me
For I knew that some would die
But to live like a man, even for a short while, is great and
  enviable
Better than a life of bars
And dogs and strikes and doles
The undistinguished private in the ranks,
As he advances up the hill,
Lives like a man

J. Gent
A Soldier of the 2nd British Infantry Division
September 1945

1. Refers to the Aradura Spur.

2nd BRITISH INFANTRY DIVISION'S RELIEF OF KOHIMA

There's a place in the east called Kohima
It's a place that we all know so well
It was here that we lost most of our manhood
And where most of our brave comrades fell

We are proud of our 2nd British Infantry Division
And the stand for freedom they made
And they swore in that place called Kohima
That Jap domination would fade

There are Taffies and Tommies and Scotties
And their flag they did fight to uphold
And that flag they will take back to Britain
And its stories, could it speak, will be told

There are men on the hills 'round Kohima'
Who will never see green British shores
But we swore in that place called Kohima,
That their souls will live for evermore

There's a place in the east called Kohima
It's a place we all know so well
And our comrades that lie in Kohima
In the glory of Britain will dwell

Anon
Royal Welsh Fusiliers
2nd British Infantry Division

THESE HANDS[1]

Beside the burnt-out remnants of this place
I saw the lifeless hands above the earth
Here then was war the horror of its face
For this, *for this*, a man was given birth

The shallow grave would scarce the body hide
Akimbo sprawled the hands were still and grey
I could not pass but knelt down by his side
To scrape the soil and cover from the day

These hands, I said, once moved and felt and knew
The warmth of other hands, and touched things dear,
Perhaps had picked firm fruit or flowers grew
Or turned bright wheels or trailed through water clear

But now no life beneath my burning touch
I tried to hide which might have been my own
Dead fingers here which once at life did clutch
But now I press them down, alone – alone

It seems so strange, the unexpected things
Which one is called to do in times like these
My mind revolves and childhood memory brings
The tears I shed, and know I cannot grieve

---

1. This poem was inspired by the death and burial of an unknown Royal Scots soldier during the Battle of Kohima. Gunner George says, "Some of their bodies had been hastily buried and it was over one of these graves I stumbled when we moved in later. The village was still burning, and I knelt and covered the exposed hands of the dead Scotsman in his shallow grave." The poem was completed that same night.

Only some deep-down pain I cannot show
Wells in my heart and floods without a sound
For this quiet heap where grasses soon will grow
For him who knows me not beneath this mound

Gunner Richard A George
99th (Royal Buchinghamshire Yeomanry) Field Regiment,
Royal Artillery
2nd British Infantry Division

YOURS

21 May 1944

Yours till the end of July sir,
Yours where the mud sticks like glue
Yours till the Monsoon goes by sir
With pants and vests sir – soaked through
Yours while the "pani" is falling
Yours "standing to" while it pours
We never loved anyone the way we love you!!
As for Kohima sir – it's Yours.

Yours with a cold on the liver
Yours with a heck of a cough
Yours from the bed of a river
Are you like us sir – browned off?
Yours "in the swim" very much sir,
Thinking of blokes still indoors,
We never loved anyone the way we love you!!
As for Burma sir – it's Yours

Reverend Kenneth W Parkhurst MBE HCF
Chaplain to 1st Battalion, Royal Welsh Fusiliers –
2nd British Infantry Division

AFTERMATH

On dread Mount Pulebadze[1] hang the clouds
Teeming with monsoon tears, they swirl and cling
Amongst the mantle of rain forest trees:
Of which the mightiest rise up through them
To form an ominous, eerie backcloth
For the frightful scene below

There stood Kohima in the Naga Hills:
A garrison with panoramic views
Spanning the fertile Brahmaputra Plain,
Through a blaze of growing rhododendrons,
To far horizons and the snow-capped peaks
Of distant Himalayas.

A far-flung outpost of the British Raj,
Set in the fastness of that mountain range
Which stands guard along the Burmese Border:
Long held to be a shield impregnable
To incursion by invading armies
But, alas, no longer so!

---

1. Mount Pulebadze is at 7520 ft. The Japanese had hauled their mountain artillery pieces up there to fire down directly onto Kohima Garrison area – they had to be taken out of action. This task was given to the only troops at General Grover's disposal who were the 2nd Recce Regiment and 143 SS Company – they did the job but the climb was undertaken in nightmare conditions with an almost vertical climb in places.

Now a sight of utter devastation
Meets the outraged gaze – the ravaged cockpit
Of a battle which has razed it to the ground;
When the rapacious Sons of Heaven sought
A crossing through the mountain barrier
To swoop down on Hindustan.

For two long months of conflict, hand to hand
Blood has seeped deep into the reeking earth
As vicious combat raged through day and night
And the dire shambles, which had once been men,
Was pulverised into the foetid mud
By mutual bombardment.

Machine gun fire has rent both the living
And the dead with murderous disregard
For any object in its flailing swathe.
Men singled out their foes with bayonets,
As oblivious as their charging boots
To the grapes of wrath, they trod

At last the weary troops have quit the field:
Some heady with relief at combat won
But others in despair because they failed,
Despite brave deed, to wrest a victory –
Thus bringing shame upon their Emperor.
(His was all the fault, not theirs)

Many, as they march away, have fearful
Dread of warfare yet to come and hurry on
To Imphal, the Chindwin and Mandalay;
Without a backward glance at what is past,
However fraught and grim their memories.
Battle ends, but War goes on!

Yet some there are whose gaze is mesmerised
By the carnage and the desolation
Amongst which they have crawled and fought like rats,
Closing their shell-shocked minds to circumstance
In order to preserve their sanity
These give thanks to have survived.

All such men will temper their survival
With thoughts of those who lie forever here,
Or lost in jungle mazes where they fell
Comrades they had entrusted with their lives,
Who died tormented deaths in pain and grief
Without complaint or rancour.

Amongst the gallant dead no victors lie,
But only sacrificial lambs to Mars,
Their offering to the fight is crucial,
Because each donation adds its quota
To the final outcome of the battle.
Living men will bear the Palms

In time to come, the few who pass this way
Will find a pleasant graveyard, neat and trim.
The Bone Collectors will have come and gone
To sanitise a peaceful place of rest.
Then some who read the serried stones may say
"So young: so many; and so far, away"

Major Douglas Messenger
2nd Reconnaissance Regt (6th Battalion, Loyal Regiment – North Lancashire)
2nd British Infantry Division

KOHIMA – HELL OF HELLS

If you read about Kohima
Or the tales you hear them tell
Of sixteen days of fighting
Those sixteen days of hell:

The boys who stopped the Jappies,
Those slant eyed yellow rats,
Who tried to march on India,
But half way met their match

It was the West Kent soldiers
Whose name is so well known
Where're they meet an enemy
They more than hold their own

So if you chance to meet these guys
Just stop and have a chat;
It's not all lies they tell you
About all this and that

They fought to save their country
From that great yellow flood
So all were free and happy
From tears and sweat and blood

They know if Nippon passed them
The outlook would be black,
So they stuck the job as ordered
And drove the hellions back

They taught the Japs a lesson
They'll remember all their days
That when they meet the West Kent Boys
They're there, and there to stay

They never ask for medals,
For glory or for fame;
They only fight for you and me
And good old England's name

Corporal R W Day
4th Battalion, Queens Own Royal West Kent Regiment
14th June 1944

Taken from *"Kent to Kohima"*

UNTITLED[1]

The little yellow perils of the Rising Sun
They tried to beat the second Div., but now they're on the run
From Kohima, down to Imphal, they were beaten all the way
And now they're still a running all the way to Mandalay

They call us Churchill's Butchers because we gave them hell
And at the great Kohima Battle over 3000 perils fell
They tried to beat the Royal Berks on Aradura and Jap Hill
But they never knew what hit them and no, they never will

And now that it's all over
And no more left to tell
I know our boys will go to heaven
And the Japs will go to hell

1. This poem was found in the back of the AB 64 part 2 (Soldiers pay book) of – 5349959 Private Arthur Webster, 1st battalion Royal Berkshire Regiment. At the bottom of the page was "Written just after the terrible battles at Kohima, Assam in 1944". It took nearly 75 years for this poem to see the light of day.

THE 2ND (BRITISH) DIVISION

The 2nd British Infantry Division were resting that day
When they got the call to join the fray
By different routes they were soon on their way
And they finished up at Kohima

Flung into an action that had to be won
They knew they were there till the battle was done
For the jap had to pay for the miles he had come
And he paid the price at Kohima

On the green covered slopes laid bare by our guns
These were the lads who had fettled the Huns
And showed to the world the best always comes
When the fight is the fight for Kohima

The tale is not, the glory not known
In this faraway place where a village has grown
The soil is now sacred, we buried our own
And planted the Cross at Kohima

The first task now over, the lads were then told
No rest for them till they'd broken the hold
On the place the jap knew was more precious than gold
The road that led from Kohima
The road is now open, Imphal is free
From second division bayonets the jap had to flee
Helped along by the artillery
Down the bloody road from Kohima

M.A. Dimmock

TO THE FOURTEENTH ARMY[1]

From Kohima to Imphal
Then on the road to Mandalay
Fought a mighty army
Thro' night and day

They pushed the Jap invader
Over hills and plains
Across the Chindwin river
And darkest jungle lanes

But oh, the cost was heavy,
The price we had to pay
In lives of gallant soldiers
Whose homes are far away

They fell for British freedom
Yet knew not, what was fame;
Men of 'The Forgotten Army'
You died, but not in vain;
Your comrades will avenge you,
And the world will speak your name

T/240993 Dvr. A.T. Bell

1. This poem was on a sheet of paper found within the Kohima Museum so it is assumed that Dvr. Bell was in the 2nd British Infantry Division.

THE SAGA OF THE MANIPUR ROAD

One by one the milestones passed
Inch by inch we fought our way
Up through the hills where our foes were massed
Fighting grimly from day to day

Here a halt and there a check
But hardly a minute to spare for rest
From the time of the dawn with its golden fleck
To the sunset glories of the painted west

Slowly indeed was the road reborn
But proud were we to give it life
Though our back were bruised and our hands were torn
With the pitiless, endless, ceaseless strife

Stubborn our foes fought, we give them due
For a rugged, reckless, bitter fight
But we showed them we had endurance too
And the certain knowledge our cause was right

Week after week they held the key
In vain we stormed the towering height
In the pale of the dawn we'd clearly see
The pitiful waste of the previous night

We licked our wounds and gazed around
But still our fears were few
For our ears were assailed with ceaseless sound
As the batteries slowly grew

Day by day, with bitter hate
They blasted a road through hell
And the score that was writ on the martial slate
Had a grey grim tale to tell

The tanks moved up in the morning gloom
And fought till the night fell fast
Full many a bunker became a tomb
Behind them as they passed

The rain came then in a cold grey sheet
And the mountain mist closed down
While the mud was churned by a thousand feet
Where the tracks led up and down

Then they fled in the night with a ten-mile start
Leaving their dead where they lay
And we followed them up with a quickening heart
In the light of the dawning day

Their rear-guard fought a savage fight
But their numbers were too few
Crushing them down with our growing might
We swept to conquests new

We dropped from the hills by the winding way
To the valley, wide and green
Where the meadow flowers were bright and gay
By the river's silver sheen

We reached the last of the milestones then
In the mountains shaded lee
And word was writ with a mighty pen
"The Road to the South is Free"

WO2 Kenneth Norman Marwood
6th Infantry Brigade
Royal Army Medical Corps
2nd British Infantry Division

NAGA LANDSCAPE[1]

Deep in the heart of the Naga hills
At dusk and the battle won
Alone in a basha midst eerie sounds
'Neath the rays of the setting sun.

Comfortless and far from home,
Though near in heart and mind
Scrub covered hills of paddy fields
The only beauty now I find

Hemmed in all round with hilltops
With their villages nestling close
To the summits of all and sundry
All alike in silent repose.

At the base o'er hill and valley
The winding road runs on
From behind the far horizon
To the midst of the setting sun.

Toiling back and forth all day
With baskets heavily laden
These dusky people staunch and true,
Old woman, man and young maiden.

---

1. "Written to my Mother from Maram Spur, Imphal Road".

   Appears as a handwritten note on the poem.

Steep khuds are naught to this clan
As up those khuds they'll go
As muscles gleam and ripple there
Such bodies proudly show.

From the road the khuds slope sharply
To the jungle stream below
A trickling thing of beauty
God willed, ne'er ceased to flow.

Beauties of nature lying
'Neath these hills of deepest blue
Though far from home and hearth dear
Natural beauties, real – like you

W.H. Greenwood

TO MY BROTHER[1]

Where e'er you are, I know you're free
God knows how much I envy thee
You did your work and did it well
Ere on your life the curtains fell

'Tis freedom we are striving for
Pray God 'tis peace for ever more
And when 'tis won at awful cost
I pray our cause will not be lost

For if 'tis lost, where is our gain?
Have men laid down their lives in vain?
Such waste of life just cannot be
They died like Him, to set us free

So fight on me with might and main
To win our freedom once again
And when the victory is won,
Our fight has really just begun

A world to build that will not err
For our children must not suffer
As we have done for one mans greed
And lust for power, o save our seed!

1. Written after Kohima, on hearing that his brother had died in the Royal Navy. Further research has revealed 2 possible casualties to fit the timing. Maurice Harold or Charles Edward Chamberlain both died in June 1944.

Build for them a world of peace
And in our struggles never cease
Until our goal is well in sight
Regain our wind resume the fight

Our freedom is our aim in life,
Freedom – from tyranny and strife
Your freedom it has won, when he
Called you to rest but yesterday

You loved by all, this I do know
Our Maker loved you more, and so
Goodbye brother, I loved you well
'Tis not goodbye, but just farewell

Bombardier Richard Chamberlain
99th (Royal Buckinghamshire Yeomanry)
Field Regiment Royal Artillery
2nd British Infantry Division

PART 6 – INTO BURMA

Even after their massive defeats at Kohima and Imphal, the Japanese still fought tenacious rear-guard actions as they retreated across the Chindwin River. Neither Slim or his Commanders realised just how badly mauled the Japanese were. Given their past experience of Japanese tactics, the Allies could not be sure that the enemy were not getting ready for a counter attack.

Allied intelligence was limited on a strategic level as well as on a theatre level by a lack of prisoners and Japanese interpreters. Planning was further held up due to Slim suffering from a bout of malaria having disobeyed his own orders not to bathe after 1800 hours and getting bitten by a mosquito. Extreme seasonal weather didn't help the Allied cause, for torrential monsoon rain slowed down any hope of close pursuit by making progress by the already exhausted troops increasingly difficult. Neither were the Japanese immune from these conditions and their soldiers were just as exhausted but the advantage lay with them as just a few of the enemy could hold up the cautious allies as they sought to catch up with the Japanese. Sickness levels rose as resistance to disease lowered due to the depleted physical condition of the men.

The 14th Army was tired but Slim knew that to hold back to allow his men time to recover would also allow the Japanese the same. He kept up the pressure and planned for a final overwhelming defeat of the Japanese Imperial Forces in Burma.

IN BURMA

When I think of sailing back to the coast
Of the land, I love in its guardian sea
This is the thing I long for most
And this is the dream that is dearest to me

To walk abroad, and to breathe again
The sweet fresh air from a Sussex hill
To find my way through a leafy lane
To a down land church so old and still

And there by the lynch- gate, to sit
In the fading light of a fair spring day
And, as the cottages' lamps are lit
To think of things at home, and pray

Reverend Kenneth W Parkhurst MBE HCF
Chaplain to 1st Battalion, Royal Welsh Fusiliers
2nd British Infantry Division

THIS SOLDIER[1]

He died, this soldier by the track
Not in the fever of some great attack
Not for the grand objective, nor the high
Gains that the jingo headlines cry

He died, without the knowledge in his heart
That dying, he would play some little part
In writing 'Finish' to a bloody tale
Seeing the dawn as he went down the vale

He died to gain no more than a mound
Unknown, unmapped – a yard or so of ground
To be abandoned when the monsoon came

He died, the touch of English breezes cold
Cold on his cheek and in his heart grown old
He died, the savour of good English earth
Faint in the fragrance, distant in its mirth

You earth that shrouds him in this strange place
Lie gently as if English, upon his face
And alone, no-one at his side
This British soldier, he died

Anon

1. This poem was found within other paperwork in the Kohima Museum without attribution.

THE CHINDWIN[1]

There's a river called the Chindwin
Running swiftly through the night
There's a railway, built by slaves
Who fought and lost the fight

There are rows and rows of tombstones
Of men from near and far
And shining o'er that scared place
A lonely Burma Star.

---

1. The only clue as to the author is the word 'Dago'. However, he is believed to be Sgt. Frank 'Dago' Davies of 16th Field Regiment Royal Artillery of 2nd British Infantry Division.

DEATH OF A SOLDIER

The jungle broods in silence, not a leaf is on the move,
No birds to sing, no animals to roar
All life has long departed from the ground and from the trees above
Escaped from this mad, man-made, thing called war

A sniper in the trees is giving trouble on the right,
If you don't keep your head down, you'll get shot
When you hear the bullet pass by, then you know you're alright
It's the soldier just behind who's had his lot

When darkness falls, remove his tags, his pay book and effects
Then wrap him in his blanket, feeling grim,
Just scrape a hole, and roll him in, a friend will then elect
To say a short sharp sermon over him

Scrape back the earth, erect a stake, to mark where he is laid
And on it cut his number rank and name
You curse the war, the enemy, the sacrifice he made
Wondering what it's for, and who's to blame.

The battle's done, advance again, we leave him in the sun
Neath his Maker, in the jungle and who knows,
We wonder if they'll find him when victory is won,
And they're put in one large graveyard, all in rows

We wonder if it's worth it, will this brave new world to be
Will it be what we hope, or just moonshine in the sky
For freedom we are fighting, but with one thing I agree
But for the grace of God, man, there I lie.

Sgt Stan Chapman
Royal Army Ordnance Corps
XXXIII Corps[1]

---

1. Royal Army Ordnance Corps units were not normally found at Divisional Level at this time.

GOD'S IN HIS HEAVEN

(The Irrawaddy crossing)

With cold indifferent hate, the guns have sown
Their instant flowering seeds of acrid dust

Black towering weeds whose searing stamens moan
For obscene consummation of their lust

And those they pierced and rent beyond recall
Renew pain transcending e'en their prior dread

And God (who sees each tiny sparrow fall)
Notes that a further hundred men are dead

Gordon Nimse
December 1944

Taken from *The Stars*

MY MULES AND I

We are off again, my mules and I
To clear the Japs, on the Silchar track
Beneath a monsoon sky
With monsoon capes, in pouring rain
Our muddy bodies heave
No piece of cake
In what it takes
To climb these hills again.

On windblown grass, the leeches wait
To share their rich delight
A shell hit mule and muleteer
Dying at first light
We are off again, my mule and I
To fight for right, in morning bright
Though none can reason why.

Private Raymond Street
Company Runner
4th Battalion, Queens Own Royal West Kent Regiment

HARRY'S[1] COMRADES

They marched into the darkness, into the unknown
They marched all together, yet each one was alone
The land which they had travelled, they knew to be Burma
Yet the only reality was Terra Firma

They were all young and confident, but a little naïve.
If they had been told, they would not have believed
The horror, the hardships, the loss, the pain
They were to suffer in the Burma Campaign

The snakes and the leeches they endured with ease
Their biggest problem was the vile Japanese
They learned to cope with the mad Samurai
The little yellow bastards who all wanted to die

They finally stopped the Jap headlong drive
And once and for all cut them right down to size
It was here at Kohima, now etched in their hearts
Where the beginning of the end actually did start.

The battle was furious, the cost was so high
The battalion fought well but a lot of them died
With courage and bayonet and cast iron will
They chased the Japanese off Garrison Hill

Bunker by bunker, by night and by day
They pushed on from Kohima and on to Mandalay
They conquered each strong point,
With bayonet and with gun
And hastened the end of the vile "Rising Sun"

---

1. It is believed that Harry was killed in action in Burma in 1944.

The ‘Forgotten Army’ of Slim’s fighting men
Who hammered the Japs again and again
They left a Memorial made of white stone
On it was a message for all to take home

The message is simple, made without fuss
WHEN YOU GO HOME TELL THEM OF US AND SAY
The ultimate is the one to obey
FOR YOUR TOMORROW, WE GAVE OUR TODAY

And still these men of the Burma Star
March together, from near and from far
They no longer march into the unknown
They walk in the Golden Light
Of the glory they have known

Bill Ridley
2nd Battalion Durham Light Infantry
2nd British Infantry Division

ODE TO THE 14TH ARMY

They loved their Scottish homeland, and English scented
lanes
They loved their great Welsh mountains and gentle summer
rains
But now they sleep in Burma, where the river Chindwin flows
A small white cross above their heads, the names their
comrades knew.
They viewed their little village streets where lights did gleam
and glow
They loved the pictures and to dance with pretty girls they
knew

They left their happy homeland, across the sea to die;
Their youth a brief glory which sped so swiftly by:
Unfurl their flag of freedom; salute your gallant sons
They came from every walk of life to fire and man the guns
They met the tyrant enemy and smashed his heathen bands
And when this war is over, and peace once more returns
We'll think of those we left behind as we watch our home fires
burn

We'll think of all those gallants neath Burma's sweating soil,
Who made the supreme sacrifice, the Japanese to foil
From Dimapur to Kohima, through Imphals bloody plain
The battle raged for many months through heat and monsoon
rain

By Tamu's steaming jungle, along the Tiddim Road
And up the chocolate staircase[1] the gallant way they strode
They rode across the frontier into Mandalay
From Fort White into Tokyo; we know no other way;
And when the 'Rising Sun' is out for good the freedom flag
    will fly
Salute the Fourteenth Army lads, they weren't afraid to die

Anon

December 1944

---

1. A colloquial name for a long winding steep road on the advance into Burma.

UNTITLED

There are fields and fields of Paddy
Round the camp at Kemeraddi
The 16th Field were stationed there as well
Though they'd been through shit and shanker
Once again, they'd dropped a flanker
By ending up in 'No-Mans' land
But in spite of lousy Kenner
It was still a point of honour
That the camp be filled with
Damsels in the nude.

Now there's one that is a smasher
To be found in Black Mikes basha
She's his joy and inspiration too
However much he'd like to ravish her
Alas she's just on paper, so his satisfaction would be
practically nil
Still that day will shortly fall
When we say, God Bless and F*** them all
From the General to the bloke who cleans the tins
Then Hi Ho for Mother Blighty
And the Missus in her nightie
They can stick the Army up their Gunga Dins

Attributed to Stan Billington
16th Field Regiment Royal Artillery
2nd British Infantry Division

THE BLOKE IN BURMA

You'll fail to find him mentioned, in the papers everyday
The news is all of Europe, and not of Mandalay
But away in far off Burma, midst the sun, the dust and the rain
There's a little chap that's fighting hard, a few mud huts to gain

He doesn't fight for prizes, like a city or a town
It's just a chaung or feature, that he's adding to his crown
And though there's no comparison, in value or in space
The odds against the little chap, are very hard to face

Today 120 in the shade, the air as still as death
Tomorrow the monsoon rains so cold, they take away his breath
Fever tears his body down, but his spirit still is game
No one reads of what he's done, but he's done it just the same

When the war is over, he'll have no awards galore
You may not even notice him, in the pub sat by the door
When others boast of what they've done, he'll smile at them
and say
"I only fought in Burma, from Mogaung to Mandalay."

Anon
A Soldier of the 2nd British Infantry Division
2nd British Infantry Division

THE FORGOTTEN ARMY[1]

These are the men that shed their blood
Among the filthy Burma Mud
On Arakan front and Imphal Plain
In blinding sun and torrential rain

This is the land of mosquito pestering
Of jungle sores with poisonous festering
Of Dysentery brought by thousands of flies
And cholera plague where one swiftly dies

Oh England[2] these are the men you forget
Think of them now as they toil and sweat
Think of the sacrifice they are making
And carrying on while their hearts are breaking

Slowly and steadily on they go
Fighting the Jap, 'a most treacherous foe'
For among this far-flung battlefield
The fate of the cunning Jap is sealed

Later on in the years to come
When you speak of battles fought and won
Remember those who fought so well
And lived and died in that green hell

Anon

---

1. Found among the effects of Lance Corporal North.
   1st Battalion Queens Own Cameron Highlanders.

2. With this reference to England rather than Scotland, it may be that Lance Corporal North was a Yorkshire Cameron!

THE HILLS OF MANIPUR[1]

The Japanese drove westward, threatening India's eastern
bounds
They swept through Burma's central plains to find new
hunting grounds.
The infiltrating intruders were confident and sure,
Until they met the friendless Naga Hills of Manipur.

Kohima was surrounded, the West Kents had to stay,
For sixteen days and sixteen nights, they held the foe at bay
Relieving troops at last arrived, the battlefield their lure,
By railway, road and air they reached the Hills of Manipur

The British Second Div. obeyed Lord Louis' distant call,
Their famous sign, crossed keys of York[2], was proudly worn by
all.
They freed Kohima's rear-guard, soon no longer had to
endure,
Then took the strain to hold the spiteful Hills of Manipur.

They fought on Dunkirk's beaches 'ere they re-equipped
anew,
They'd left the shores of Britain in the spring of 'forty-two.
Well trained in multi purposes for reasons yet obscure,
They got a tough assignment in the Hills of Manipur

---

1. In the interests of accuracy, it is pointed out that the Battle of Kohima was not actually fought in the Hills of Manipur but in the Hills of Assam.
2. See explanation of the Crossed Keys

Five thousand feet above the sea Kohima Ridge stood proud,
And often like its neighbouring peaks was capped with clammy cloud.
The British warriors feeling strange, remote and insecure,
Maintained their struggle for those treacherous Hills of Manipur.

They fought against fanatic foe and mother nature's frown,
They fought in endless seas of mud as monsoon rains poured down.
They'd jungle sores and leeches, strange diseases, no prompt cure,
But their orders were to clear the cruel Hills of Manipur.

The japs were flung from every hill and blasted from their trenches,
With furious fighting, hand to hand, midst horrid scenes and stenches,
The once all-conquering enemy now fled from his pursuer,
But brave young lives were lost in those sad Hills of Manipur.

Message reads "when you go home, tell them of us and say',
And follows on 'For your tomorrow, we gave our today'.
These words are carved upon a stone where heroes sleep secure
In tidy graves, amid the peaceful Hills of Manipur,

Bombardier Maurice Wood
16th Field Regiment Royal Artillery

Written at Kohima but taken from *Keynotes 2000*

HEROES[1]

Heroes sleeping, softly lying
'Neath soil for which you fought.
Sleep on, your rest in Heaven assured
This soil was dearly bought.

Deeds that echoed round the world
Were yours and truly earned
A place for you in history
Such things not easily spurned

Serious the situation was
As o'er Indian soil you rushed
The Jap o'er the frontier hurrying was
Assured and with victory flushed.

To stem his might and hold him
Kohima was named the place
Where you, brave fellows met him
Picked then of a gallant race.

From Dimapur he'd nearly reached
Slowly your power gained sway
Up through Zubza and beyond
To Kohima where he meant to stay.

But you didn't think the same as he
As you dug into the 'khud' side
Only to move him whatever the cost
Regardless of numbers who died.

---

1. Because of references within the poem, it is assumed the author to be 2nd British Infantry Division.

For forty odd days, this battle raged
For a tiny Assam town
Time battalions shared attacks
Two Div. was ne'er let down.

Once the Jap was on the run
How easy it was to keep him
O'er hill and dale and the winding road
Pursued by you good men of Shin.

Imphal had been besieged for weeks
But you chased him miles beyond there
Over the ghats and through Samum
To end up only God knows where

Anon

THE FOURTEENTH ARMY

They have gone past, men of the shield and sword[1]
Last of our fame, and half the world away
From all familiar things; so let them rest
Now that the battles done. The jungle way,
From Naga Hill and over Chindwin's banks
Will hear no more their green limbed stealthy tread,
Or watch with fevered eyes where tanks have gone,
And little boats, and where a man lies dead.
Across their airlines blow the purple clouds,
Water and grass and nameless twilight things
And where their voices whispered, silence clings
An army passes, but its loves remain,
Freedom – and a way home through jungle rain

Lockhart Howell

1. Refers to the insignia of the XIV Army

MANDALAY

In the land of shining Pagodas
At the time of Nipponese fame
Came a Division of British soldiers
To put old Nippon to shame

We met him first at Kohima
Much to old Jappy's regret
Then we kept him in quite a dilemma
Right through to monsoon so wet.

The Jap we found was good in the hills
But we soon had him taking a few of our pills
From morning till night, we were moving along
To the strain of the pipes or an old folk song

But soon came the Chindwin and the river Mu
And then the old 'Waddy'[1] came slap into view
Our pace never slackened right on thro' the fray
And we freed the old city of quaint Mandalay

Anon[2]

---

1. Refers to the Irrawaddy River
2. From notes on the original this poem is attributed to Sgt Johnny Johnson after action at Mandalay

A SOLDIERS MOON[1]

The curtain clouds roll back, their thunder spent
And rain-washed mountains to the east appear
Against the evening sky, so sharp and clear
Across the cool sweet air, and jungle scent.
Moon mounting, soon to dominate the night
A star beckoning each soldiers view
Towards his jungle rendezvous

There comes the copper moon disc, burnished bright
I turned my eyes away from soldier's moon
To sunsets afterglow, from thought of war
To ask, as I have often asked before
And ask each eventide – how long – how soon?
For you are in tomorrow's unborn day
Beyond the sunset, half a world away

Anon

1. Found on single sheet of paper within the Kohima Museum. Written on rear of sheet – "sent to me from Burma by Sgt Thomas" signed by "Scottie"

PART 7 – REMEMBRANCE

Not all of the poems were written during the war. Many of the veterans put pen to paper in their twilight years as memories of those fearsome times began to resurface, if indeed they had ever been buried. Advanced years is often a time for reflection and these men certainly had enough to reflect upon. Memory might fade as to precise detail but the feelings of dread and fear would remain clear as would the sight of comrades dying in brutal circumstances. As previously mentioned, the writing of the poems and recollections was cathartic.

Despite this therapeutic effect, some of the poems just cannot hide the hatred that still prevailed for the Japanese.

REMEMBRANCE

For a bereaved friend
The years may come and go...
Alas so fast,
But memory sets aglow
A cherished past.
Though loving has its cost
And thus we wept
For all that we have lost,

Reverend Kenneth W Parkhurst MBE HCF
Chaplain to 1st Battalion Royal Welsh Fusiliers –
2nd British Infantry Division

SEA REQUIEM

The sea bell tolls for time across the tide
It does not call us to a holy place
But God is here, where wind and wave confide
That prayers rise up with the simpleness of grace
Within my heart I hear the ringing call
The deep and plaintive longing of the soul
Still searching for the truth surrounding all
The pattern and fulfilment of the whole

Strange how this bell creates some hidden fears
A slow and solemn note as old as time
The muffled beating measured in long years
A requiem that cries for all mankind
I hear a bell repeat some ancient rite
And stand transfixed within the fading light

Gunner Richard A George
99th (Royal Buchinghamshire Yeomanry) Field Regiment, Royal Artillery
2nd British Infantry Division

THE DREAMS OF AN OLD KOHIMA MAN

I very often dream of Kohima
I have for the last 50 years
And the terrible things that I dream of
Have always reduced me to tears
It's not very big is Kohima
Little tin huts and shacks
But it took a terrible beating
From all those Japanese attacks

When the monsoons came to Kohima
You thought things just couldn't get worse
Your blood is being sucked by the leeches
And you rant and you rave and you curse
You think things couldn't get worse in Kohima
But I think I'm telling a lie
Because the next attack the Japs make
It could be your turn to die

Tonight, I'll dream of Kohima
My wife says, "did you have a good night?"
But I couldn't even tell her
I've been sweating all night with fright
Please don't even ask me
Why I did all those terrible things
Because there in my head when I'm dreaming
The hatred just rings and rings

I just could not tell anybody
The way I hate Japanese
Because the pain in my head and the hatred
Just brings me down to my knees
You know it's really quite funny
To have all these thoughts in my head
I wasn't raised to be violent
Because shooting and killing I dread.

One night I may dream of Kohima
And over the township I'll fly
And hover like a big eagle
With the sun, up there in the sky
It's now been such a long time
Of hating and feeling the pain
Of the time that we fought at Kohima
In the mud, the heat and the rain
I think it's about time now
That god came up with a plan
To end the suffering and nightmares
Of this old Kohima man

Fusilier John Done
1st/8th Battalion Lancashire Fusiliers
Attached 143 Special Service Company
Headquarters 2nd British Infantry Division

MIRACLES

Miracles occur each and every day,
The opening of one flower to the light
The sun's uprising on its measured way
The starlit beauty of ensuing night

An oak tree growing from an acorn sees
A cobweb, gem encrusted, with dewy grace
The tidal ebb and flow, so sure indeed,
They move with mystic love, through time and space

Miraculous, the marvel of all birth
A unique star in a galaxy of snow
A rainbow's beauty, arching over the earth,
The egg's enigma, we may never know

There is no doubt, that miracles abound,
Into each life they lovingly surround

Gunner Richard A George
99th (Royal Buckinghamshire Yeomanry) Field Regiment, Royal Artillery
2nd British Infantry Division

KOHIMA'S UNSEEN CASUALTIES[1]

Night unfolds her velvet mantle
The wind plays with the falling leaves
Her sad eyes through the panes unseeing
By the window softly grieves

Her thoughts return to summer meadows
To their wedding day and honeymoon
His photo on the bedside table
Share memories in her lonely room

A small voice from the doorway calling
Mummy, why are you standing there?
Can I come and sleep in your room?
Can I bring my teddy bear?

That's a picture of my daddy
I can't remember him at all
Did he rock me in my cradle?
Did we play with my red ball?

Tell me more about my daddy
Why did he go away so soon?
Sometimes, did he pretend to toss me
Far higher than the moon?

---

1. Taken from a sermon read by The Chaplin General The Reverend Dr Victor Dobbin at the Kohima Memorial Service – July 1997.

Your daddy went to be a soldier
And he had to go far away,
He loved us both, so very much
And sent his love each day

Now close your eyes my pretty one
And say your evening prayer
God bless daddy – mummy too
And my Teddy bear

Little eyes now close in sleep,
God Bless – I know He will
Your daddy sleeps beside his friends
Sleeps on Kohima Hill

Anon

A TRIBUTE TO THOSE OF KOHIMA

In the heat and through monsoon
They could pay the pipers tune
For their courage was unequalled- even there
Where the Chindits went before
These men added to their score
And they won a battle honour with great flair –

Kohima was its name, and they earned undying fame
In the jungles and the deserts, as of yore.
Now, as years roll by, our pride
In those who fought and died
In their efforts to stem the tides of war

The FAITHFULS[1] paid the price
In the land of teak and rice
They made their mark, for all to see
In the glory of their dead
The battled on ahead
Played a part out east, to set all Nations free

John Allan
2nd Battalion, The Durham Light Infantry
2nd British Infantry Division

1. This is a nickname of the Durham Light Infantry. During the Battle of Kohima, they fought a furious and vicious battle to retake Kuki Picquet, in which they lost 98 men killed, wounded and missing, including 9 officers.

WHY

Why do we weep
Why do we cry
Those boys asleep
They had to die
And since that day
The Cross Keys say
For your tomorrows
We gave our todays

Attributed to Sgt Frank 'Dago' Davis
16th Field Regiment Royal Artillery
2nd British Infantry Division

SUPPLICATION TO MARS

Dread god of war, whose kingdom stretches far
Across the world; and for whose sake have bled
Thousands and thousands, Frenchmen, Russians, Japs
Italians, Greeks and Germans; who has led
His willing slaves to slaughter; who delights
To see the streams of earth run red, blood red,
We would worship thee, would to thee proffer
All our flesh and bones and blood; would suffer
All things for thee, till all thy lusts are fed
But alas, we have no blood to offer
Will whitewash do instead?

J. W. N.

UNTITLED

No doubt you've heard of Libyan sands
And Italy's Terra Firma
But have you heard of the really bad lands
Of Assam and Northern Burma

Those are the lands of the jungle deep
Of swamps and blood sucking leeches
Where lives everything that god made creep
And only experiences teaches

Those are the lands where the fittest survive
And the weak just fall by the way
Where they fed us on tablets to keep us alive
And sweat poured from us all day

Where snipers lurked amongst the trees
And every hilltop sheltered a gun
As we scrambled up on our hands and knees
To exterminate the Japs of the rising sun

There were no roads, just jungle tracks
Where mules were known to falter
But men carried on with loaded packs
Through mud and stagnant water

There were no towns to liberate
No Civvies to cheers us on
Just millions of insects to irritate
And the jungle rolled on and on

So when you read of what Britain wrought
On Europe's plains and beaches
Just spare a thought for those who fought
Mid jungle swamp and leeches

Anon

THE DAY IS ENDED

The sinking sun in golden glory
Bids a weary world to rest
Eventide, the same old story
Lonely thoughts turn west

As the sun is slowly sinking
'Midst the twilights purple hue
Treasured thoughts each man is thinking
Thoughts, awaking dreams anew

Light and shadows softly blending
Spreads a mantle over all
Heralding that day is ending
Warning us that night must fall

In those moments of the twilight
Precious moments all too few
Hovering t'wixt dark and daylight
Sacred moments spent with you

Dark the night and long the day
Dame fortune's gifts are few
So with Eventide I pray
"God send me back to you"

Steve

AT THE CROSS

Step up before me child, so I
Can hear your name.
Thank you for the flower, dear
Please tell me why you came.

"Grandma had to see you, she thinks of you every day,
She tells me all about you, but I know not what to say".
"Nanny kept a photograph, and I have seen your face,
She keeps you on the mantle, it takes up pride of place".

"Daddy has had your medals, since he was a lad,
He remembers when you went away,
And the good times that you'd had".
"So you see we are all here, on this glorious day,
We keep you in our thoughts and hearts, you're never far away."

Rob Aitchison

IN GRATEFUL DEDICATION

Ours is a “today”
Dearly ransomed in blood
That freely flowed “yesterday”
A sacrifice, the whole
This tennis court was too poor to contain

Gallantly lay they their lives down
What price, what price a soul
For the fair Kohima

To her, O faithful dead,
You can never, never die
While you live on in our hearts
And generation to generation repeats
The story of your sacrifice

May the skies never close over you
May the rains woo you softly,
The mountains be hushed before you
May you rest in eternal peace

Easterine Kire[1]

---

1. Easterine is an established poet and author. She was born in Kohima and remembers as a child how her mother and grandmother used old 3-inch mortar ammunition containers to cook their Christmas puddings in. Her uncle was the first Kohima War Cemetery Superintendent.

THE UNKNOWN SOLDIER

Why does no one pause at my grave
After all, I too was brave.
They pass me by and kneel and pray
At a nearby grave or across the way.

I also fought for what was right
And here I lie by day and night.
Is there a reason they pass me by?
If there is, please tell me why.

I turned away with puzzled mind,
The answer to his words to find.
Then I looked upon the stone,
A gallant soldier, Name Unknown.

So, remember if you pass his way,
Pause awhile to chat and pray.

Cyril W Crain[1]

1. From the sheets this poem and others were written on, it is believed that this author was a soldier of the 2nd British Infantry Division.

HAVE YOU HEARD

Have you heard of a place called Burma?
The land of forgotten men
Who fought in a steaming jungle
Against the ferocious army of Japan

Have you heard of the Royal Navy?
The Royal Air Force as well?
Nor forgetting the merchantmen
Who served in the campaign too.

Have you heard of the Burma railway
Built by these very men
Many of them died in the effort
But some of them did survive.

Have you heard of the town of Kohima
On a hill nearby stands a rock
On which is carved this epitaph
And this is what it reads,

WHEN YOU GO HOME
TELL THEM OF US AND SAY
FOR YOUR TOMORROW WE GAVE OUR TODAY

Jim Kelly

FIFTY YEARS

Fifty years have come and gone
The Burma Lads still carry on
With eyes now dim and legs so weak
With creaking bones and aching feet
We still get there with sticks or chair
Proud to say that 'We're still there'

We came home, they had to stay
And lie forever where they lay
No more they'll see the light to fade
Or smell the flowers in the jungle shade
Nor hear the birds sing on their grave
Suffer no more from the life they gave
We're proud to say that "we were there"
But they forever will be there!

Anon

ENGLAND MY ENGLAND[1]

What has happened to our England
The flag held so high in dignity, the love sincere and bold.
What has happened to our England
The centuries of strength, patriots of old?

We move to lose identity in international schemes
To forfeit independence and our island way of life,
To be part of Europe, beyond our wildest dreams
A conquest of deception without an act of strife

Wake up and blow bugles in every English shire
To rouse complacent English folk to look ahead and see
A sense of new commitment to set the heart on fire
With noble thoughts that England is forever free

Great Britain is dismembered by thoughtless little men
Oh! Hear proud voices calling from the power of the past
Rise up! Resist! Have faith that we are great again
That England is triumphant to preserve the truths that last

What has happened to our England
The glories that were ours, the heritage that we knew,
What has happened to our England
The fortitude of spirit, that faith so deep and true?

Gunner Richard A George
99th (Royal Buckinghamshire Yeomanry) Field Regiment, Royal Artillery

---

1. Written in 2005, this poem by Gunner George reflects his political feelings, rather than his memories of those days in the Arakan, Kohima and beyond.

GOING HOME

We are the soldiers, the men without glamour
Six years we've had of it, training and waiting
Training and fighting, fighting and resting
We have learnt to distrust those above us
We believe only in the present

We have known bleak boredom, great frustration
We have trained like athletes for the race
but it was cancelled.
We have been entered at the last minute, un-warned,
Into the bloody lists of slaughter

We have learnt to hate
To shoot the starving enemy as our duty
Bodies and minds are tougher, sensibility deadened
Nerves are worn out, emotions long thwarted.

Now after nearly four years we prepare to return
What good will stay with us, six years' soldiers?
This bond will remain, outweighing all evils
All things we have shared, both hardship and pleasure

Some we have lost, not unavenged.
But we who remain and return will ever remember
The pride of our comradeship forged by the long years of war

Anon
South East Asia Command 21st October 1945

I REMEMBER

Kalewa[1] and Kalemyo
Are names which ring a bell
Tiddim, Le -U, Kohima,
I remember just as well

I remember those I flew with
As though just yesterday
The friends I lost remembered to
They'll never go away

Flight Lieutenant (Ret'd) Alan M Blackburn MBE, RAF
31 Squadron RAF[2]
Gunnery Leader

Former Trustee of the Kohima Museum

---

1. These are names of towns in Assam, Manipur and Burma where the British & Indian troops benefitted greatly from the courage and bravery of these men from the Royal Air Force

2. Although not strictly 2nd British Infantry Division, the RAF synchronised their attacks with the ground troops to great effect and success

VJ DAY AUGUST 16th, 1945

Gin tinkles merrily in glasses
We have won the war
Self-preservation is complete
Happy banter and laughter
We can return to our loved ones

On a jungle hilltop in Kohima
Bleached bones lie barely buried
Bones of our comrades
White crosses parade in military rows
In Shwebo cemetery

Was there an ideal?
Our sons will not be slaves
But freedom is not fulfilment
If there is not a turning away from self
There will be war, no peace

Anon

Written near Secunderabad, India

MEDALS

Go and pin your medals on
Be proud they're yours to wear
Pull your shoulders back a bit
And let the youngsters stare
They are yours by right of war
For service to the crown
They are symbols that you
Did not let your country down
Wear them proudly on your chest
And let who will deride
They are yours by right of war
So carry them with pride

Desmond Burgess

Taken from *The Stars*

TO MY SON

I think that all is quiet where you are lying,
The smoke and dust of battle long since gone,
Now little birds and shy small animals come freely
About their daily life, while you sleep on
When the light of day touches the hilltop
Folding away the mist that evening laid
With careful hands to shield you from the darkness,
That you might rest there safe and unafraid;
One shining ray will light where you ae lying,
Spreading its radiance like a flag unfurled,
A memory of the glory of your passing,
And of the courage that you gave the world

Anon (a Mother)

Taken from *The Stars*

MY DAD CRIED ON REMEMBRANCE SUNDAY[1]

He didn't take long to prepare
A cup of tea, the TV, sat in his favourite chair
At 11, he stood to attention, straight and erect
It was his way of showing them respect
My Dad cried on Remembrance Sunday

Were they tears of joy; no
Tears of regret; maybe so
Tears of gratitude for he made it home
Tears of sorrow for those left buried alone
My Dad cried on Remembrance Sunday

It doesn't take long to prepare
A cup of tea, the TV, sat in my favourite chair
At 11, I stand to attention, straight and erect
It's my way of showing him respect
It's my turn to cry on Remembrance Sunday

Are they tears of joy; no
Tears of regret; maybe so
Tears of gratitude for he made it home
Tears of sorrow for I now watch alone
It's my turn to cry on Remembrance Sunday

Robert Street
Kohima Museum Trustee

---

1. Written in memory of his dad Private Raymond Street – 4th Battalion Queens Own Royal West Kent Regiment. Although not 2nd British Infantry Division, the 4th RWK came under command of 2nd British Infantry Division for the duration of the Battle of Kohima.

PERCY'S THOUGHTS ON 'THE RETURN TO KOHIMA'

The Jungle blooms, it lives again, the wildlife wanders free,
The village children sing again, there's blossom on each tree,
But o'er the hill past the tennis court a silent graveyard lies,
And as I stand and reminisce, the tears come to my eyes.

Once again, I hear the noise of battle being fought,
The cries of men in agony, this land was dearly bought,
I see again the bungalow, where men fought and died,
The scene it lingers with me still and fills my heart with pride.

Kohima Ridge is peaceful now, the sun is burning bright,
But I see only battlegrounds where we fought, wrong with right,
I proudly read the 'Epitaph' and slowly bow my head,
A salute to all my comrades, a prayer for all our dead.

And as I leave Kohima, those friends, I leave behind,
They stay because they died for us, for us and all mankind,
They'll never be forgotten, nor the words that clearly say,
"For your tomorrow, we gave our today"

Percy Goulden
Southport Branch
Burma Star Association

A WAY OF LIFE

Out in the hills round Kohima,
A war to end wars was fought.
The road that led to Victory,
With many dangers was fraught.

But the men who died in this battle,
In jungle green were dressed.
Their webbing and boots weren't polished,
Nor were their trousers pressed.

They dined when they could on Bully,
And with their fingers they ate.
And a dirty old issue mess tin,
Served instead of a plate.

They had no use of a napkin,
Their fingers were wiped clean on the grass.
They didn't drink wine from lead crystal,
But drank water and thanked god for that.

The way that they lived was no filly,
But circumstance was to blame.
They lived rough because they had to,
In so doing there was no shame.

I should have no need to tell you,
The facts that I've mentioned here.
We all lived the same in the jungle,
Let's admit it without any fear.

So when we remember our comrades,
With a dinner and dance, or a ball.
Remember we were just plain soldiers,
With no frilly bits at all.

Our members are not all counted workers,
But that's no fault of their own.
And others have suffered from sickness,
And some misfortune have known.

Please consider these facts very carefully,
When planning 'A Do' or 'A Ball'.
And try and arrange things better,
Not just for some, but for all -

Percy Goulden
Southport Branch
Burma Star Association

AFTER WAR

And shall these years be now in vain,
Shall the torment, suff'ring, pain
Be but the father of another Cain?
It cannot be!

Shall all that you and I have done
Shall all that peace so hardily won
Be but as transient as the setting sun?
It will not be!

Shall husband separate from wife?
Shall children, born to peaceful life,
Find that they have a heritage of strife?
It must not be!

This is the problem facing you,
This is the work *we* have to do
So, let us steadfast pledge ourselves anew
It *shall* not be!"

Anon

Taken from *Keynotes*, January 1944

THE NORFOLK CROSS

On a hill far away to the south of Mandalay
Stands a simple wooden cross to our dead
They were brave as they fell,
In that God forsaken hell
Everyone a hero as he fought and bled

We will look up to that old wooden cross,
And remember our comrades who died,
We will cherish the old Norfolk cross,
As we stand here and sing side by side
The Old Norfolk Cross

Anon

This Memorial to the Royal Norfolk Regiment has been erected on land reputedly purchased by the Regiment itself. This land is now used by the local Naga people for a number of purposes although the immediate area around the memorial remains clear.

FEVER SONG

And did you serve in India lad,
Or Burma's wild green land?
And did you have the fever there
Till you could scarcely stand?
And does the fever catch you still
When England's winds blow bitter chill?

And does your head throb once again
As it did then, my lad?
And do you feel the dulling pain
The same as you once had?
And do you, soldier, curse the day
When under those hot sky's you lay?

And do you shake and shiver, lad,
And ache to lay you down,
As you did then, short years ago,
Under the jungle's crown?
And do you sigh for water now,
And drink the salt sweat from your brow?

And do your limbs feel far away
In agues sudden grip?
And do you like the price you pay,
The fever cup you sip,
For being young in England's Isle
When Hitler saw his war god smile?

Or do you think of well-known friends,
Men of your Company,
Who, uncomplaining, met their ends,
Nor looked for sympathy;
But under Asia's brassy skies
Died with this England in their eyes?

Their rotted bones in jungles lie
Six thousand miles away –
Lad, what's a fever? you won't die.
You'll live to fight another day –
But God forgive, if you forget
They paid, in agony, our debt.

Kitty Hutchinson (nee Jones)
Queen Alexandra's Imperial Military Nursing Service
East Grinstead 1947

COMRADESHIP

Comradeship is a lovely thing,
If shown in the proper way.
No matter what your station,
You'll need a friend one day.

As I lay wounded in Burma
With a hole where my groin should have been
In a slit trench that served as a theatre,
My leg was patched up and made clean.

It was there that I saw real friendship,
From men more hurt than I.
And as I remember that friendship,
Tears of thanks fill my eyes.

A man with no legs passed me water,
A man with no eyes passed a smoke.
And one with no hands gave me comfort
And one with no arm gave me hope

All who have served in Burma
Know and understand
That the greatest gift that God gave man
Was a friend at either hand.

Who'd break a cigarette in half,
So you could have a smoke.
Or give you his last Anna,
If he thought that you was broke.

But these are only earthly things,
That man can well afford.
But comradeship goes further,
In the eyes of Christ our Lord.

If you want the proof of this,
Just stop and think awhile.
Remember all our comrades,
Among the rank and file

Think of all they gave for us,
All those who had to stay.
For all our tomorrows,
They gave their today.

This then is true comradeship,
But we don't have to die.
Just to prove our friendship,
Or keep our morals high.

Just show again the comradeship,
We had in days gone past.
Our comrades will rest happy,
Their job is done at last

Percy Goulden
2nd British Infantry Division
Southport Branch
Burma Star Association

THE OLD INSIGNIFICANT MAN

When he walks down the street
You may know him
He could be old Charlie or Dan
When he walks past your door
He may be old bent and poor
Yes, an old insignificant man

When he tells of the past
You should listen
Of the terrible thing in the war
His tales are not very nice
He stops and thinks twice
This old insignificant man

He will tell of the pain and the suffering
It takes him so long to tell
Of the killing he did and the hatred
And the thoughts that go through his head
When he fought a sadistic enemy
From Italy, Germany and Japan
These are the stories he will tell you
This old insignificant man

His body may be battered and broken
He may have a mentally affected mind
That's why he wants to tell you
Of the comrades, he left dead behind
This is just part of his story
It's not the end of the plan
He wants you to understand the problems
Of an old insignificant man

Fusilier John Done
1st/8th Battalion Lancashire Fusiliers
Attached 143 Special Service Company
2nd British Infantry Division Headquarters

ARADURA SPUR

Where are the old men with silvery hair?
They were forgotten and the world didn't care
They were the young men with memories to share
They who fought and died on Aradura Spur

They fought in a battle that was not very good
On a small piece of land monsoon rain running with blood
God was not looking or did he just not care
When he let this carnage happen on Aradura Spur

You may not know them there were so many kinds
With their broken bodies and tormented minds
Those with so many memories to spare
The fighting young heroes on Aradura Spur

When you go to your churches to kneel and say prayers
Stop for a moment if you have one to spare
And just say a few words
For those brave young men from Aradura Spur

Fusilier John Done
1st/8th Battalion Lancashire Fusiliers
Attached 143 Special Service Company
2nd British Infantry Division Headquarters

KOHIMA 1954

Returning to Kohima ten years after the battle[1],
I was guided to my battalion's memorial
By a ten-year-old barefoot boy.
As he trotted up the track which the bulldozer[2] had driven,
Now a leafy lane,

He explained the bullet-riddled corrugated iron
And the grass-filled foxholes.
Having led me to the place I wanted to be,
He scampered off
To re-join his playmates.

Later, in the cemetery,
I walked along the endless rows of headstones,
Learning not to move too slowly,
Which can cause tears,
Nor yet too fast,
When numbers dull the sense of individual tragedy.

---

1. This experience of 10 years after the Battle, stayed with Gordon Graham and led to him founding, together with other 2nd British Infantry Division Veterans, the Kohima Educational Trust in 2004 to honour the people of the Naga Hills who had given the British unstinting support, at great cost to themselves, during the Battle.

2. A bulldozer had been used to force a track of a steep incline with sharp bends in order for a Mark 3 Grant tank to get up and blast the Jap bunkers.

Next morning I rose while it was dark
And went for a walk in the jungle,
Seeking ghosts,
But finding none.
As I stumbled through the thickets
In the mist of a rainy dawn
A bugle sounded reveille.

At that moment, I understood
That life is a partnership
Between the living, the dead and the unborn,
And that we, the living,
Have the duty
To pass to those who follow us
The wisdom and ideals
Of those who have gone before us.

Major Gordon Graham MC and Bar
1st Battalion Queens Own Cameron Highlanders

Major Graham was one of the founding Trustees of the Kohima Museum when it originally formed in 1989.

THE DAKOTA

The battle was won through dogged weeks:
flying low; with kicking feet,
The troops below there to supply
With precious rations from the sky.

Bravery and credit due,
To both the air and ground crew too,
Thereby whose courage victory rose.
Through dropped supplies on chutes did flow.

'Forgotten war' is what it's called,
So far from roads to reach them all,
The troops below held all in thrall,
Time will endure to remember them all.

Terence P. O'Halloran
Curator 31 Squadron Association

PART 8 – THE FINALE

The Reverend L.E.M. Claxton MC – Chaplain to 2nd Battalion The Dorsetshire Regiment at Kohima, gave an address at York Minster in on the occasion of the 50th Anniversary of the Battle of Kohima which included the following:

> "...I buried a friend on a hill so remote that the Graves Registration Unit couldn't find the grave. They were wonderful in doing a difficult job of bringing everybody in, and this was the only time they had to call on me to act as a guide. He was young, devoted to his wife and little daughter, and I found a notebook in his breast pocket and a prayer:

Only one favour would I ask of God: Give me, Oh God,
And give to those I love the days we missed

Also in his notebook was this poem:

O you who live in England
You will never, never know,
How we long to be in England,
Breathe the scented air of England
See the timid daffodils
That wander to and fro,
When Spring takes hold of England
Kissing all the land
O you who live in England
You will never understand

Dear Friend, I can't answer your prayer: but I promise you this. While any of us in Kohima are here under the sun – we will gather together and remember you..."

It has now been established that the friend referred to was Captain Michael Morice, 2nd Battalion Dorsetshire Regiment who was killed on 28th May 1944 and is now buried in Kohima

At the going down of the sun,

and in the morning, we *will* remember them

BIBLIOGRAPHY

Books

Burma Star Association, Boston & North Cambridgeshire Branch, *The Stars: Anthology of Poems* Richard Kay Publications 1990

Carstairs, Peter R. *So this is India – A Few Impressions of a New Country.* Self-published in India 1943

Calver, D. H. *Padre Pastor & Poet – Reverend Kenneth W Parkhurst MBE HCF 1907 – 1987* Self-published 1988

Slim, Field Marshal Sir William, *Courage and Other Broadcasts*, Cassell & Company Ltd 1957

South East Asia Command (SEAC) *Laugh with SEAC.* Locally-published in India 1945

Stanley, Major E. B. & Tillott, Major A. T. *From Kent to Kohima,* Gale & Polden 1951

Other Publications

2nd British Infantry Division *Keynotes*, fortnightly Divisional newsletter published between March 1943 and March 1944

South East Asia Command, *SEAC, Daily Newspaper of South East Asia Command* 10 January 1944 – 2 December 1945. Printed in Calcutta

The Sunday issues are entitled *Sunday SEAC*

INDEX OF FIRST LINES

THE CROSSED KEYS

At the outbreak of WW2, the British Army's 2nd Division was commanded Major General Charles Henry Loyd. He took the Division out to France, fought it there and brought it back from Dunkirk. Before his promotion to Major General, Loyd had commanded 1st Guards Brigade which had as its 'flash', a single key. When he received his second 'Star', it felt entirely appropriate simply to add another key to the one he had had before. Thus by this minor administrative gesture, the 'Crossed Keys' division was born. In design the new emblem for the 2nd British Infantry Division was a pair of white crossed keys on a square black background.

After the Division was repatriated from Dunkirk it was headquartered in and around York and ever since, there has been a degree of myth and misunderstanding surrounding the emblem's origins. Some have said that it came about because of the historic fact that Britain's 2nd Army was always raised in the North under the banner of the Archbishop of York, while others have maintained that the Crossed Keys of St Peter (York Minster) was the influence. A further 'connection' occurred when the Division, upon completing its tour as part of the Occupation Force in Japan following the end of the war in the Far East, was relocated to Germany as part of the British Army of the Rhine (BAOR) in 1947. In the late 1950's, The Division's headquarters was moved to the north German town of Lübbecke, which also has the crossed keys as its symbol, also from St Peter, this time from the parish of Stockhausen, in which the town sits. By this time, of course, the crossed keys had already been its emblem for many years.

with the coincidences of the 2nd British Infantry Division being stationed in a succession of locations with strong connections to the Crossed Keys of St Peter actually having no bearing on the selection of the emblem whatsoever.

And there is another small coincidence connected with the Kohima Museum and the Division. Following the battle, as the Division advanced along the Kohima-Imphal road, its leading elements met their equivalents of IV Corps, coming towards them from Imphal at Milestone 109. The museum has been housed in Building 109 in Imphal barracks almost from its inception.

SECOND BRITISH INFANTRY DIVISION - ORDER OF BATTLE 1944

Royal Artillery

10th Assault Field Regiment
16th Assault Field Regiment
99th (Royal Buckinghamshire Yeomanry) Assault Field Regiment
100th (8th Gordon Highlanders) Light Anti-Aircraft/Anti-Tank Regiment

Royal Engineers

5 Field Company
21 Field Park Company
208 Field Company
506 Field Company

Royal Signals

2nd Divisional Signal Regiment

Divisional Troops

2nd Bn Reconnaissance Regiment Royal Armoured Corps [6th Bn. Loyal Regiment (North Lancashire)]
2nd Bn Manchester Regiment (Divisional Medium Machine Gun Regiment)
143 Special Service Company
387 (DUKW) Company RASC

4th Infantry Brigade

1st Bn. The Royal Scots (The Royal Regiment)
2nd Bn, The Royal Norfolk Regiment
1st/8th Lancashire Fusiliers

5th Infantry Brigade

7th Bn. The Worcestshire Regiment
2nd Bn. The Dorsetshire Regiment
1st Bn. The Queens Own Cameron Highlanders

6th Infantry Brigade

1st Bn. The Royal Welch Fusiliers
1st Bn. The Royal Berkshire Regiment
2nd Bn. The Durham Light Infantry

Divisional Support Troops

Royal Army Medical Corps

4th Field Ambulance
5th Field Ambulance
6th Field Ambulance

Royal Army Service Corps

8th Brigade Company
24th Brigade Company
29th Brigade Company

Royal Electrical Mechanical Engineers

2nd Divisional Workshop

Other Formations Under Command

33rd Indian Infantry Brigade from 7th Indian Division

1st Bn. The Queens Royal Regiment (West Surreys)
4th/1st Gurkha Rifles
4th/15th Punjab Regiment

161st Indian Infantry Brigade from 5th Indian Division
(Formed original garrison defending Kohima during the stage of the siege)

4th Bn. Queens Own Royal West Kent Regiment
1st/1st Punjab Regiment
1st/7th Rajput Regiment
24th Mountain Regiment. Royal Indian Artillery

Royal Air Force (In Support but not Under Command)

31 Squadron
34 Squadron
84 Squadron

AUTHOR BIOGRAPHIES

Robert Melville Cook

Born in 1948, Bob joined the British Army as a Boy Soldier in 1964 and served for 34 years as a Royal Signals soldier. He ended his military service at Imphal Barracks in York as a Warrant Officer and bought a Guest House near the Barracks. In 2008, he volunteered to take over as volunteer curator to the Kohima museum and with a small team of other volunteers transformed the museum into a modern dynamic museum which showcases the stories of the men of the 2nd British Infantry Division who fought with Major General J.M.L. Grover CB, MC. He has since taken this small museum through a number of phases of Accreditation under the guidelines of the Arts Council of England. Bob is the 4th and latest Curator since the formation of the Kohima Museum. He is also a Trustee of the Kohima Educational Trust.

Robin McDermott, MSc, MA, AMA

Born in 1946, Robin was commissioned into the British Army in 1966, and served for 30 years as a logistician. During the last 7 years of his service, whilst serving in a succession of posts on the staff of the Second Divisional Headquarters in York, he established the Kohima Museum in Imphal Barracks, to act as a formal repository for the increasing quantity of memorabilia donated to the Division by the veterans of the Battle during their annual reunions. Following his military retirement in 1996, he re-qualified as a museum professional, engaged in the intimate support of all museums in the Yorkshire region in their efforts to acquire, and subsequently maintain, compliance with the nationally-based museum minimum standards scheme. Since his final retirement in 2011, he has returned the fold of the Kohima Museum by being appointed as one of its trustees.